Mt. Ararat
16,946 Ft.
Araxes R.
Caspian Sea
Lake Van
Lake
ASSYRIA
Nineveh
Zab R.
R.
MESOPOTAMIA
Ashur
ZAGROS MTS.
Euphrates R.
Tigris R.
Babylon
AKKAD
BABYLONIA
Nippur
SUMER
Lagash
Shushan
ELAM
ARABIA
Ur
Eridu
CHALDEA
Persian Gulf
MILES
0 50 100 200 300

The Continuity of the Bible

Joshua to Elisha

Also by Thomas Linton Leishman

The Continuity of the Bible: The Patriarchs

Our Ageless Bible — From Early Manuscripts to Modern Versions

The Bible Handbook (with Arthur T. Lewis)

Why I Am a Christian Scientist

The Interrelation of the Old and New Testaments

THOMAS LINTON LEISHMAN

The Continuity of the Bible

Joshua to Elisha

THE CHRISTIAN SCIENCE PUBLISHING SOCIETY

BOSTON MASSACHUSETTS, U.S.A.

These articles appeared in
The Christian Science Journal
during the period 1966–1968

Library of Congress Card No. 71–87144

Printed in the United States of America

Preface

In a published collection of articles dealing with "The Continuity of the Bible," originally appearing in the pages of *The Christian Science Journal,* it was natural that the opening volume should be subtitled "The Patriarchs," dealing as it did with the great founders and early spiritual leaders of the Hebrew people.

"Continuity" naturally suggests continued progress and indeed the purpose of this volume is to indicate progress and unfoldment. The concept of continuity as we consider it is not necessarily limited to chronological order but applies rather to development of thought, including the upward trend of such thought towards the New Testament.

The basic work of the Patriarchs, as outlined in the preceding volume, entitled *The Continuity of the Bible: The Patriarchs,* now leads on to the consideration of an established and developed government in the Promised Land of Israel. The work of the Patriarchs themselves was essential. They prepared the way for progress.

Abraham, his son Isaac, and his grandson Jacob had joined in laying a firm foundation. The years which the people of Israel spent in Egypt supplied not only a period of testing and trial but also a time of deep significance. Joseph provided a clear indication of the Hebrews' capacity for government by his extraordinary success when serving as Pharaoh's prime minister.

With Moses, the spirit of freedom unfolded, and under the guidance of God he presented the necessity of Moral Law in the form of the Ten Commandments. Moreover, under Moses' leadership and that of his successor, Joshua, their people were freed from the physical and mental bondage of Egypt.

In this, the second volume of this series dealing with the establishment of the Hebrews in their own land of Israel, we see the concept of a nation grow along many lines. Joshua's leadership shows his perpetuation of Moses' ideals in a new environment.

With the coming of the Judges, the increasing need for rulership became evident, while the career of Samuel forecast the necessity of a stable government supported and upheld by the ideals of prophecy, which meant so much to him, acting as he did as judge, prophet, priest, and reformer, all in one.

While Samuel's anointing of Saul as Israel's first king proved to be far from an unmixed blessing to his subjects and even to himself, at least it established monarchy as a possible, if not always an ideal, method of rule. Saul's successor, David, who was anointed by Samuel, proved to be more stable and effective in his practice of kingship; while the wealth and energy of David's son and successor, Solomon, contributed to the establishment of Israel as virtually a world power. Still Solomon's royal state had its limitations, and with his passing his mighty empire quickly broke down into two relatively small and insignificant kingdoms — Judah in the south and Israel in the north of Palestine — each with a separate king.

A higher and more spiritual form of unity was needed, not based merely on material progress or royal state, but rather upon spiritual advancement and loyal devotion to the one true God of Israel in a wider and more ideal sense.

Samuel the prophet, in his own life and work had envisioned something of the essential value and significance of prophecy; further, with the coming of Elijah and Elisha, the stress on kingship gradually diminished, and prophecy became increasingly important along many lines of endeavor.

These great seers of the ninth century B.C. based their work upon the recognition of the essential rule of God Himself, claiming and proving through Him the basic power of healing and of harmony in contributing to the progress of their generation.

Of almost equal value seems to have been their work of encouraging eager young prophets in contributing to the sources of the Pentateuch — Genesis to Deuteronomy — thereby preparing for the vital significance of Hebrew history, where law and prophecy often proceeded hand in hand.

True, Elijah and Elisha seem not to have left written records of their messages of true advancement, healing, and salvation in their own words, but they indubitably prepared the way for the literary prophets of the Old Testament.

Certain questions may arise as the reader of this volume and the preceding one tries to relate their contents to the order of the books as found in the Old Testament.

In attempting to outline "The Continuity of the Bible" as if it were one book, it is not always either practical or advisable to discuss each separate Biblical book individually or in detail or in its traditionally published sequence. The *Torah,* or Law of Moses, is generally taken as finding its basic expression in what is often termed the *Pentateuch,* literally "five-fold volume" — Genesis to Deuteronomy. These books were compiled, scholars agree, from numerous different sources, often coming from widely differing periods. Moses was the predominant figure in these five books rather than necessarily being the actual author of each book, as the individual headings might suggest.

A somewhat similar problem arises when studying the First and Second books of Samuel, of Kings, and of Chronicles; which, while apparently providing historical records of the kings, prophets, and others, whose lives are discussed in them, were evidently set down by various, and often unnamed, scribes or recorders. It is as difficult to determine the precise dating of these books as it is to identify their authors.

In the reference to the career of Solomon, one of the most famed kings of Israel, it has not been practical to try to describe in detail the numerous literary efforts often associated with his name.

Because of the wisdom repeatedly attributed to this king in the Old Testament and occasionally in the New, it was usual among the Jewish people to claim that not only was he the author of The Song of Solomon but also of the books of Proverbs and of Ecclesiastes.

It may be added that most scholars are inclined to date all three of these books from a period many centuries after the time of the historical Solomon, but this would not rule out their interest and significance. Whether or not Solomon personally composed them, they may well have been written in his vein of thought, as implied in other portions of the Bible.

While such noted leaders as Ezra and Nehemiah, who worked largely in Jerusalem during the period following the end of the Babylonian Exile, are not considered as contributing directly to Hebrew written prophecy, they do seem to have supported the activities of such prophets as Haggai, Zechariah and others, and so would naturally be mentioned in connection with them. Similarly, the book of Esther includes events corresponding in time to some of those in the book of Daniel, considered the latest of the Old Testament prophetic books.

T. L. L.

Greenwich, Conn., April, 1969

Contents

MAPS

CHAPTER I ·

Joshua's Leadership in the Promised Land

Joshua and the Fall of Jericho

Moses' passing on the summit of Mount Pisgah marked the conclusion of the forty years of Israelite wandering. Although he had not been permitted to enter Canaan, Moses had been shown from afar the land originally promised to Abraham's descendants. Joshua, who had been trained to succeed Moses, was now placed in full command by God, who declared: "As I was with Moses, so I will be with thee: I will not fail thee, nor forsake thee. Be strong and of a good courage" (Josh. 1:5, 6).

Quickly responsive to this challenge, Joshua proclaimed that within three days the Israelites must be prepared to cross the Jordan and claim their inheritance (see Josh. 1:11). Doubtless recalling that he himself had been one of the spies originally sent forth to survey the land of Canaan when the people had first approached it many years before, he now sent forth two men to investigate the situation in Jericho, the first large city within Canaan. There they encountered Rahab, a woman described by Josephus as an innkeeper, who provided not only lodging but also encouragement and protection, reporting that the men of her city, having learned of the successes of the Israelites and of the support afforded them by their God, were virtually paralyzed because of fear and could do little to resist the attack planned by Joshua. Assuring Rahab that she and her family would be protected as a reward for her cooperation, the spies returned to report the success of their mission (see Josh. 2).

Thus encouraged, Joshua took immediate steps to plan the crossing of the Jordan. This passage was clearly viewed not merely as a military stratagem, associated with the conquest of the land, but also as a religious act. The people were to sanctify themselves (see Josh. 3:5) and were to be led by their priests, who would reverently bear "the ark of the covenant of the Lord" (verse 11), symbolic of God's presence and leadership. Moreover, when this maneuver commenced and the feet of the leading priests touched the water, there was virtually a repetition of the experience which had encouraged the Israelites some forty years before when they had passed dry-shod through the Red Sea (see Ex. 14:29).

On this present occasion, in spite of the fact that the river was in flood (see Josh. 3:15), the priests, with their precious burden, together with the Israelite host following closely in their footsteps, crossed on dry ground, showing that the conclusion of the Exodus was as surely protected as was its commencement. As a reminder of this deliverance, twelve stones from the Jordan were preserved, one for each of the twelve tribes, as "a memorial unto the children of Israel for ever" (Josh. 4:7).

The first great event following the passage of the Jordan was the capture and destruction of Jericho. Here again the ark of the Lord took an important part in the fulfillment of Joshua's God-ordained plan. For six successive days the ark was carried around the city, accompanied by seven priests carrying rams' horns, and by the "men of war" (Josh. 6:3). On the seventh day this circuit was made seven times. On the final circuit, at a signal from Joshua, all the people accompanied a long trumpet blast with a mighty shout. The walls of Jericho "fell down flat" (verse 20), and the people marched over them to victory.

Much work had still to be done, but the first major conquest in the Promised Land had been accomplished.

The Apportionment of Canaan

Flushed with their success in capturing Jericho under Joshua's leadership, the Hebrews were convinced that a smaller force would be ample to overcome the city of Ai (see Josh. 7:3), but to their dismay they suffered a crushing defeat. Turning to God for an explanation of this reversal, Joshua learned that it stemmed from the disobedience of Achan, who had stolen for his own use from the rich spoils of Jericho, spoils either consigned to destruction or dedicated to God's service (see Josh. 6:24; 7:11–13, 19–21). After the punishment of Achan, and the renewed dedication of Israel to obedience, Ai was overcome by means of a stratagem (see Josh. 8:1–28).

Typical of Israel's successes in southern Canaan was their effective defense of their allies, the Gibeonites, from the concerted attack of the armies of five Amorite kings. Even the forces of nature appeared to assist the Israelites (see Josh. 10:11–14), while city after city fell before them.

For a time the northern provinces remained unconquered, but the backbone of their opposition was broken when Israel decisively defeated another confederacy led by the king of Hazor, in spite of the reputed invincibility of his armies (see Josh. 11:4).

Now that the greater part of Palestine was under his control, Joshua proceeded to its apportionment among the Hebrew tribes. Naturally, he acceded readily to the request of Caleb, one of the staunch leaders of the tribe of Judah (see Num. 13:6), that he might have the territory surrounding Hebron. Joshua doubtless recalled Caleb's strong support of him when the two men had urged the advance into Canaan almost half a century earlier (see Num. 14:6–9). At that time Caleb had shown no trace of fear at encountering the giant "children of Anak" (Num. 13:28), who lived near Hebron. Now, although he was "fourscore and five years old" (Josh. 14:10), Caleb was ready and eager with God's help to overcome his enemies.

At this point Joshua gladly confirmed the allotment which Moses himself had given to Reuben, Gad, and the half tribe of Manasseh so that they might have the territory to the east of the river Jordan. In spite of the inheritance assured to them in this area, these tribes had agreed to support their brother Israelites in conquering the land to the west of the river, meanwhile leaving their families and their stock in the eastern province of Gilead (see Num. 32:25–33).

The territory to be assigned in western Palestine to the remaining nine and one half tribes was granted by casting lots under the supervision of Joshua, as Moses had planned (see Josh. 14:2). In the southern section, Judah received the extensive territory bordering the shore of the Dead Sea and close to the land surrounding Hebron, already ceded specifically to Caleb. Simeon received ground south of Judah, which was soon merged into Judah's territory (see Josh. 19:1, 9). Benjamin was located north of Jerusalem, and between it and the Mediterranean lay the acreage assigned to Dan.

Ephraim held a central position south of the ground allotted to the western half of Manasseh's tribe, which stretched between the Mediterranean and the Jordan. Issachar was bounded by Manasseh on the south and the river on the east. What was later called Galilee contained Zebulun in the south, Asher in the northwest, and Naphtali in the northeast. Joshua himself received "the city which he asked, . . . Timnath-serah, in mount Ephraim" (Josh. 19:50).

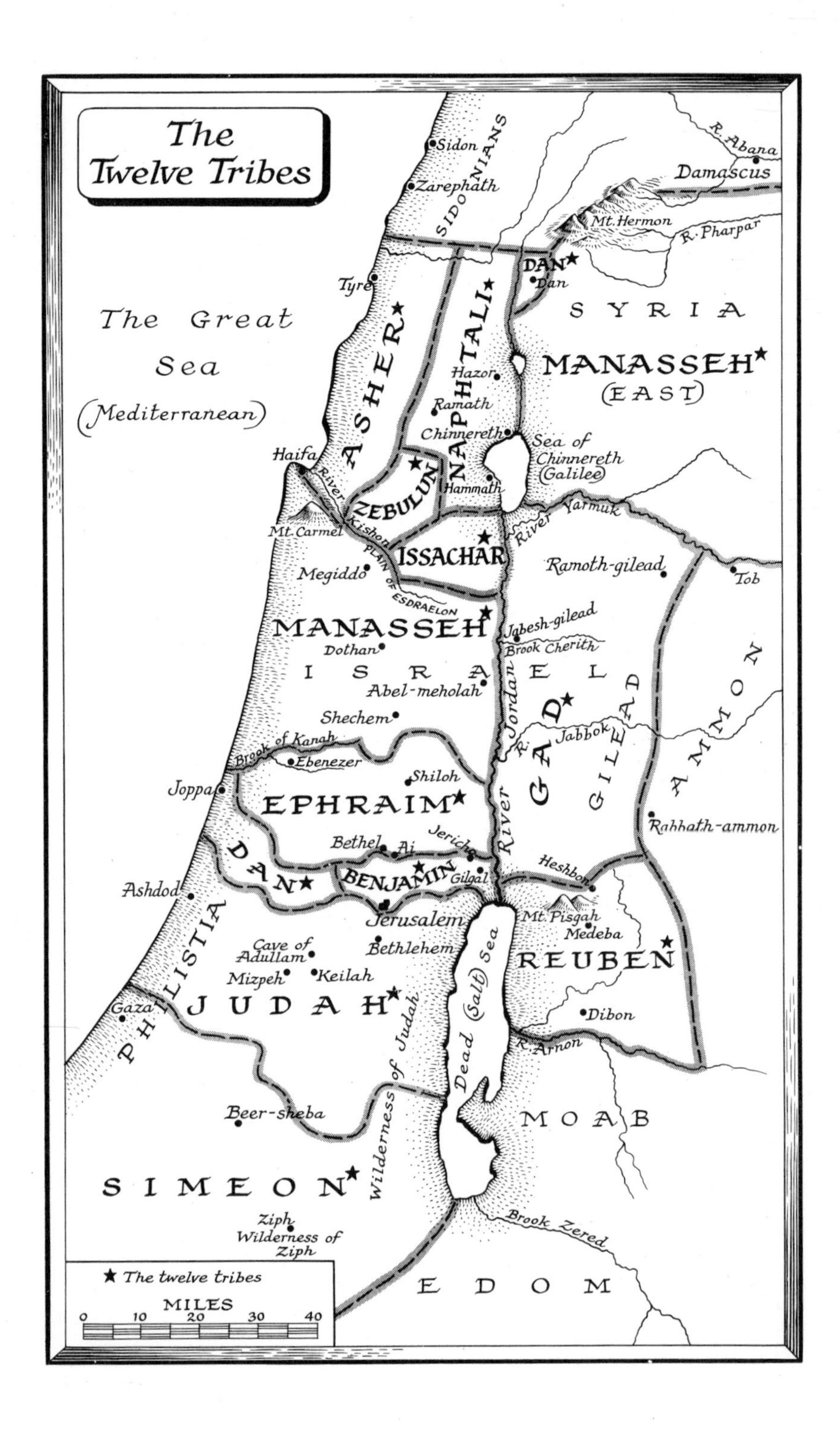

The Twelve Tribes
The Great Sea (Mediterranean)
Sidon
Zarephath
SIDONIANS
R. Abana
Damascus
Mt. Hermon
R. Pharpar
Tyre
DAN
Dan
SYRIA
ASHER
NAPHTALI
MANASSEH (EAST)
Hazor
Ramath
Chinnereth
Sea of Chinnereth (Galilee)
Haifa
River Kishon
ZEBULUN
Hammath
Mt. Carmel
River Yarmuk
ISSACHAR
Megiddo
PLAIN OF ESDRAELON
Ramoth-gilead
Tob
MANASSEH
Jabesh-gilead
Brook Cherith
Dothan
ISRAEL
Abel-meholah
AMMON
Shechem
GAD
Jabbok R.
GILEAD
Brook of Kanah
Ebenezer
River Jordan
Joppa
Shiloh
EPHRAIM
Rabbath-ammon
Bethel
Ai
Jericho
DAN
BENJAMIN
Gilgal
Heshbon
Ashdod
Jerusalem
Mt. Pisgah
Medeba
PHILISTIA
Cave of Adullam
Bethlehem
Dead (Salt) Sea
REUBEN
Mizpeh
Keilah
Gaza
JUDAH
Dibon
R. Arnon
Wilderness of Judah
Beer-sheba
MOAB
SIMEON
Ziph
Wilderness of Ziph
Brook Zered
EDOM
★ The twelve tribes
MILES
0 10 20 30 40

CHAPTER II ·

The Period of the Judges

The Era of the Judges

Following the settlement of Canaan, brilliantly outlined and executed by Joshua, Moses' associate and successor, plans had to be made for the government of the loosely knit Israelite tribes, which at this stage of their development were still largely family units, bearing allegiance to the memory and leadership of the patriarch Jacob.

During the wilderness period, Moses had encouraged them, but also held them in check, establishing their basic laws and recalling them constantly to loyalty toward their God. Under Joshua they saw the glowing dream of the Promised Land become a reality; but, as yet, they were largely nomadic in character, not ready for the responsibilities of settled citizenship and established monarchy — a type of rule later associated with such royal rulers as Saul, David, and Solomon.

These early years in Canaan were transitional, representing in a measure a time of colonization or, perhaps, of Israel's adolescence. When eventually Joshua's strong hand was removed by his passing, there was a tendency toward anarchy among the people whom he had led so effectively. "In those days there was no king in Israel, but every man did that which was right in his own eyes" (Judg. 17:6).

It was about this stage in Israel's experience that "the Lord raised up judges" (Judg. 2:16), as recorded early in the book of Judges; and indeed what occurred in "the days when the judges ruled" (Ruth 1:1) is of no small importance to the student of Hebrew history and religion.

Later chapters will discuss the activities of some of the more significant of the twelve or more individuals described as judges in this portion of the Old Testament, but at this point it is important to consider the basic implications of the Hebrew word *shophetim,* or judges.

These individuals were not strictly judges, in the modern sense of the term, implying magistrates or officers of justice, although one of them, "Deborah, a prophetess," is reported to have "judged Israel" under a palm tree (Judg. 4:4, 5). The primary mission of these successive judges was both to rule and to deliver the Israelites, saving them from the dangers and humiliations following their all too evident practice of idolatry and other acts of disobedience to God. It is clearly indicated that God Himself selected the judges as a consequence of His mercy and in response to the prayers of the Hebrews; and we are assured that "the Lord was with the judge" (Judg. 2:18).

If the book of Judges be read in the sequence of its recording, it becomes evident that there is to be found an oft-repeated cycle of events which is sufficiently uniform to demand comment. This in no way implies that the book is to be dismissed as unhistorical in character. Rather it appears to indicate that historical events were set down in a consistent design to stress more clearly the moral and spiritual lessons presented by these recurring events.

Time and again we note this sequence: The sin of Israel is followed by its punishment, leading to Israel's prayer to God; in response He sends a judge or deliverer who conquers their enemies; whereupon peace ensues. Typical instances of this constructive sequence are found in the third chapter of Judges, which records the deliverance wrought by Othniel over the Mesopotamians (see verses 5–11), and by Ehud over the people of Moab (see verses 12–15 and 27–30).

Deborah

The book of Judges lays special stress upon the significance of Deborah, who, in addition to judging or delivering the Israelites, acted in the capacity of a prophetess (see 4:4). After twenty years of repeated attacks inflicted on her people by Sisera, commander-in-chief of the armies of Jabin, king of Hazor, whose territory lay in the far north of Canaan, Deborah's most memorable work began.

Under her brave and incisive leadership careful plans were made for the destruction of the Canaanite forces. Not only did she enlist the competent aid of Barak, the son of Abinoam, to muster the armies of Israel, but she also called upon Jael, the wife of Heber and another staunch Amazon like herself, to hold a key position in her plan.

Deborah convinced Barak that God would be with him and would ensure the success of their cause; and she readily agreed to accompany him into battle (see Judg. 4:9). She called upon him to recruit ten thousand men from the tribes of Naphtali and Zebulun, which were situated between her own headquarters near Bethel and those of the Canaanites at

Hazor to the north of the Sea of Galilee. Moreover she assured Barak, doubtless through her prophetic inspiration, that the decisive battle which she envisaged would be held in the immediate vicinity of the river Kishon, which to this day flows through the Plain of Esdraelon into the Mediterranean close to the modern seaport of Haifa. And with reference to Sisera, the Canaanite commander, Deborah said to Barak, "I will deliver him into thine hand" (Judg. 4:7).

It was not long before Deborah's prediction was fulfilled to the letter. The battle was fought near Megiddo and by the river Kishon; and despite Sisera's "nine hundred chariots of iron" (verse 13) and a great host of men whom he brought, the fortunes of war were against him from the start. The Canaanites were decisively defeated and destroyed; in fact, the Bible expressly states that "all the host of Sisera fell upon the edge of the sword; and there was not a man left" (verse 16).

At this point the role which Deborah had assigned to Jael was specifically fulfilled. Seeking to escape from the rout of his army, Sisera had sought to gain sanctuary in Jael's tent and apparently felt that he was welcomed there; but as he slept, exhausted by the fray, Jael slew this enemy of her country, thus completing the defeat of the Canaanites.

The events of this momentous day in Israel's history are also recorded in the fifth chapter of Judges, which is commonly described as the song of Deborah and Barak and preserves what many consider to be some of the earliest passages found in the Old Testament — passages presumably contemporary with the events set down. It was indeed a song of gratitude and triumph, praising God for His goodness and His support, and noting how even the forces of nature were on the side of Israel: "The stars in their courses fought against

Sisera. The river of Kishon swept them away. . . . So let all thine enemies perish, O Lord: but let them that love him be as the sun when he goeth forth in his might."

Forty years of rest and peace succeeded this signal deliverance; but they were to be followed by Israel's renewed disobedience to the laws and decrees of God; for, as later judges found, Israel had not yet learned her lesson — the necessity of consistent and permanent obedience.

Gideon

Gideon is one of the outstanding judges mentioned in the book of Judges as delivering the people from danger or oppression. His preparation seems to have been more along agricultural lines than along political or military ones, for he was threshing wheat on his father's farm when he received this assurance: "The Lord is with thee, thou mighty man of valour" (Judg. 6:12).

While acknowledging God's previous deliverances of Israel, Gideon admitted that he could see little proof of such protection in his own day, for the roving Midianites, "as grasshoppers for multitude" (verse 5), were ravaging the country, destroying livestock and crops alike. But he was reassured that the Lord would be with him, in spite of, or perhaps because of, his humble plea of personal inadequacy. Through him, the thrall of the Midianites would be broken.

The first task assigned to Gideon was a specific challenge to idolatry. His father, Joash, had erected an altar to the Canaanite deity Baal and had set up beside it what the King James Version terms a "grove" — now generally viewed as a carved wooden idol or symbolic pole. In obedience to a divine command, Gideon destroyed the altar and used the wood of the pole as fuel for burning a bullock in honor of the Lord. Thus he braved the wrath of his neighbors, who threatened him with death. However his father stood by him, observing sarcastically that if Baal's honor had been violated, it was his responsibility to vindicate it for himself if he were indeed a deity.

Meanwhile the Midianites and other hostile tribes had amassed an army to destroy Israel's forces now rallying to Gideon's standard. At this point, Gideon's army numbered thirty-two thousand men; but a message from the Lord assured him that this number must be reduced lest the forthcoming victory be attributed to human, numerical success rather than to divine support. Any soldiers showing a trace of fear were to return home at once. Twenty-two thousand took advantage of this opportunity, reducing the army to ten thousand.

One further test remained, for God said, "The people are yet too many" (Judg. 7:4). At a nearby body of water the test was carried out. All but three hundred men disregarded caution and responsibility and kneeled down, burying their faces in the cool water and drinking to their hearts' content. The remainder, alert and ready to meet any emergency, stooped only long enough to scoop up a scant supply of water to quench their thirst. These three hundred were alone chosen to represent Israel.

Learning that the Midianites were already fearful of the outcome of the battle, Gideon divided his men into three groups and equipped each man with a trumpet, a torch, and an earthenware jar to shield its light temporarily. During the night he stationed his men strategically around the Midianite camp. At midnight, following a prearranged signal, all broke the jars and held up the lights; they sounded their trumpets and raised in unison the battle cry, "The sword of the Lord, and of Gideon" (Judg. 7:20). Their foes were demoralized and fled, even attacking one another.

It is noteworthy that there appear to have been no casualties among the three hundred stalwarts of Israel, even though they pursued their enemies for many miles.

Following Gideon's signal victory, he was offered the seemingly rich reward of hereditary kingship, but he refused it, saying to the Israelites, "The Lord shall rule over you."

Jephthah

Following its description of the outstanding work performed by Gideon, the book of Judges records briefly the activities of various minor individuals who delivered Israel from time to time. It lays stress upon the important contribution of Jephthah in meeting the needs of his times, in spite of the opposition, unkind criticism, and domestic tragedy which fell to his lot.

Gideon had encouraged and inspired his compatriots; but as time went by, they lapsed into idolatry. Such apostasy brought about dire consequences, expressed through the oppression of the Ammonites. In this new emergency the Israelites offered verbal repentance to the Lord, only to learn that this was insufficient. Indeed it was not until they manifested active reformation, "put away the strange gods from among them, and served the Lord" (Judg. 10:16) that they discovered a champion already in their midst, Jephthah, "a mighty man of valour" (11:1).

During his early days in Gilead, to the east of the Jordan River, Jephthah had been widely scorned as "the son of a strange woman" (11:2), and, somewhat like David at a later period, he became the successful leader of a band of outlaws in the vicinity of Tob, not far from Gilead.

Anticipating an attack by the Ammonites upon the forces of Israel, the elders of Gilead ignored the way in which they had once contributed to the expulsion of Jephthah from his home and from his land and now demanded that he be their captain and leader. They promised him complete authority if only he would help them in their time of need. Although well aware of the unreasonableness of their approach, Jephthah agreed to accept their plan.

Despite his military tendencies, Jephthah's first step on assuming command was to seek to settle the dispute with the Ammonites by peaceful negotiation. It was only when that effort signally failed that he and his forces attacked their enemies, gaining, with the Lord's help, a decisive victory.

Then Jephthah encountered the tragedy of his success. Before going into battle, convinced that "the Spirit of the Lord" (11:29) had come upon him, he had rashly vowed that if God brought him success, he would sacrifice to Him, as a burnt offering, the first living thing he might encounter on his return home. This thing turned out to be his daughter, his only child. So he broke the sixth commandment of the Mosiac Decalogue in an endeavor strictly to obey the third one.

Jephthah had still further trials to encounter; for the men of Ephraim, who had been saved and protected by the victory which he had won at such cost to his personal happiness and peace, now denounced him for allegedly failing to enlist their support in the campaign. Jephthah reminded them of his request for their aid, which had met no response. Civil strife ensued all too quickly. The Gileadites captured the fords of Jordan, employing as a password the term "Shibboleth." They knew that no Ephraimite seeking to return to the western bank could pronounce Shibboleth correctly but would call it Sibboleth, thus revealing his identity as an enemy.

Jephthah's six-year judgeship demonstrated his desire to do God's bidding as he understood it. His effort to resort to arbitration rather than to war revealed a surprisingly enlightened approach; but when war proved to be inevitable, he decisively defeated the enemies of his country.

Samson

The story of Samson, whether based entirely on fact or resulting in part from the embellishments of hero worship, still retains many elements of permanent interest and value. His fantastic deeds of almost superhuman prowess (see Judg. 15:4–6, 15; 16:3, 29, 30) may have the quality of folklore, but interwoven in the account is information concerning Hebrew history and custom that cannot be classified as mere legend. Moreover, as both a Nazarite and a judge, Samson merits serious consideration.

Like Isaac and Samuel in the Old Testament and John the Baptist and even Jesus in the New, Samson was a child of promise. His mother, the wife of Manoah, who came from Dan on the borders of Philistia, had long been childless, but "the angel of the Lord" announced that she would bear a son (Judg. 13:3). Not only was her son to be raised as a Nazarite, but she herself, during her period of pregnancy, was to be subject in some degree to the strict Nazaritic regulations, such as refraining from eating any food considered as technically unclean and from drinking any intoxicating liquors or any product of the vine, whether fermented or otherwise. The basic requirement of the Nazarite vow (see Num. 6:1–21) was complete devotion to the service of God. The further demand was that the Nazarite's hair must never be shorn.

With Samson's birth there came renewed indications of the nature of his work, that of delivering "Israel out of the hand of the Philistines" (Judg. 13:5), and of the divine guidance awaiting his acceptance, for the Lord blessed the child, and soon "the Spirit of the Lord began to move him at times in the camp of Dan" (verse 25).

Few Biblical characters ever received as auspicious auguries concerning the nature and fulfillment of their careers as did Samson. But as time went by, his flamboyant successes were all too often marred by sensuality, his phenomenal physical strength by weakness of character.

The first indication of Samson's involvements with Philistine women, in spite of the fact that the Philistines were the mortal enemies of his country, appears in his eagerness to wed "a woman of Timnath" in Philistia (Judg. 14:1). His parents not unnaturally opposed his desire, not realizing that it was part of a divine plan to defeat the Philistine forces (see verse 4).

Eventually, Delilah, another Philistine with whom Samson had become involved, betrayed to her people what he considered the secret of his strength — the typically long hair of the Nazarite. When it was shorn, his strength departed. The Philistines bound and blinded him, shamefully displaying him in the temple of their alleged deity, Dagon.

At length awakened to the necessity of prayer, Samson successfully besought God to return his strength. Crumbling the central pillars of the pagan shrine, he destroyed not only himself but also more than three thousand of Israel's enemies.

A man of great promise, who "judged Israel twenty years"

(Judg. 16:31) and presumably sought to fulfill the lofty obligations of a Nazarite, Samson is reported to have been aided repeatedly in his career by "the Spirit of the Lord." While he abrogated many of his opportunities by bizarre and uncalled-for exploits and by his weakness where women were concerned, he proved the power of prayer and was listed among the heroes of faith honored in the New Testament (see Hebr. 11:32).

Ruth and Naomi

Closely associated with "the days when the judges ruled" (Ruth 1:1) in Israel is the vivid account recorded in the book of Ruth, in which the leading characters are Ruth herself and her mother-in-law, Naomi. Although Naomi and her husband, Elimelech, came originally from Bethlehem in Judah, they and their two sons, Mahlon and Chilion, had settled in Moab to the east of the Dead Sea, and the two young men had married Moabite wives, named Ruth and Orpah respectively. In due course both Elimelech and his sons passed on, leaving Naomi and her two daughters-in-law. This situation sets the scene for this idyll of constancy and loving cooperation.

When Naomi decided to return to the land of her birth, Ruth and Orpah offered to accompany her; but while Orpah was eventually dissuaded from doing so, nothing could shake Ruth's determination and touching constancy. "Intreat me not to leave thee," she cried, "or to return from following after thee: for whither thou goest, I will go; and where thou lodgest, I will lodge: thy people shall be my people, and thy God my God. . . . The Lord do so to me, and more also, if ought but death part thee and me" (Ruth 1:16, 17).

Together Ruth and Naomi made their way to Bethlehem, arriving there at the start of the barley harvest. There they settled in the vicinity of an estate owned by a wealthy farmer, Boaz, a close relative of Elimelech, Naomi's husband. Eager to do all that she could to contribute to the meeting of Naomi's needs, Ruth offered to glean in a nearby field following the reapers.

During her first day in the field, Ruth unexpectedly encountered Boaz himself, who had already learned of the deep loyalty of this young Moabite widow to her Judean mother-in-law. "The Lord recompense thy work," he said, "and a full reward be given thee of the Lord God of Israel, under whose wings thou art come to trust" (Ruth 2:12). Moreover Boaz cooperated with her in every way, urging her to continue gleaning in his field until the harvest was over and arranging for his men to permit her to glean more than a normal amount of barley.

Learning that it was Boaz himself who had proved to be Ruth's benefactor, Naomi lost no time in reminding her that, as she put it, "The man is near of kin unto us, one of our next kinsmen" (Ruth 2:20).

Noting the growing attraction between Boaz and Ruth, Naomi suggested that Ruth appeal to an ancient Hebrew custom that if a man died childless, as had Ruth's husband, Mahlon, his brother or his nearest male relative should marry his widow. While readily admitting his responsibility in this matter, Boaz explained that there was another relative closer to Mahlon than he; but he added that if this man would give up his right, Boaz would gladly assume it (see Ruth 3:1–13).

At the gate of the city, the traditional spot for making legal agreements, the arrangements were concluded. The nearest kinsman, in the presence of witnesses, did relinquish, in favor of Boaz, his prior right to marry Ruth by ceremonially removing his shoe; while Boaz confirmed the agreement and purchased from Naomi the property of Elimelech, Mahlon, and Chilion (see Ruth 4) — not to mention Ruth herself.

In due course, Ruth gave birth to a son, named Obed, and through him Boaz and Ruth became the great-grandparents of King David.

CHAPTER III ·

The Rise of Samuel

Samuel the Boy Prophet

One of the more significant and versatile characters in the long record of Israel's history was Samuel, whose brilliant career affected many aspects of the progress of his country and of its people. Not only did he judge Israel "all the days of his life" (I Sam. 7:15), but he became equally well known as a counselor of kings. His activities as both priest and prophet were widely acclaimed.

His father, Elkanah, was of priestly descent, tracing his ancestry back to Jacob's son Levi, and lived at Ramah, not far from Jerusalem (see I Sam. 1:1, 19).

On one of his annual visits to Shiloh, some fifteen miles distant from Ramah, Elkanah was accompanied by his wife Hannah, who had long remained childless — a condition then considered not merely a misfortune but even a disgrace. Eagerly she offered her prayer at the sanctuary that she might have a son. She vowed to dedicate him exclusively to God's service if only her request were granted, as indeed it was within the year. No wonder she "called his name Samuel, saying, Because I have asked him of the Lord" (I Sam. 1:20).

No sooner had Samuel been weaned than Hannah took him, young as he was, to Shiloh, where "the child did minister unto the Lord before Eli the priest" (I Sam. 2:11). Each year when she and Elkanah made their annual visit to the sanctuary, Hannah took Samuel "a little coat" similar to the long robe often worn by men of authority, such as prophets, priests, or rulers. Quickly the boy endeared himself to the aged priest Eli, who came to love him as a son (see I Sam. 3:16). Eli's own godless sons had proved to be a bitter disappointment to their father (see I Sam. 2:12).

The Bible records a beautiful and familiar description of the call which came to Samuel from the Lord Himself. True, from early boyhood he had been serving in the temple under the tutelage of Eli, but here we learn that "Samuel did not yet know the Lord, neither was the word of the Lord yet revealed unto him" (I Sam. 3:7). His age when his call came is not recorded in the Bible, but according to Josephus, Samuel was a lad of twelve at the time.

The King James Version notes that "the word of the Lord was precious in those days; there was no open vision" (see I Sam. 3:1); or, as Moffat says, "A word from the Eternal was rare in those days; visions were not common." But with Samuel, a new light dawned.

Four times in succession God called to the boy by night until at length, prompted by Eli, Samuel replied, "Speak; for thy servant heareth" (verse 10). The message which came to his ears was stern indeed, announcing the utter downfall of the house of Eli. It must have been hard for the lad to report such news to the aged priest, but he did so, obediently and accurately.

This revelation marked the beginning of Samuel's great mission as a prophet. There was now even more positive evidence of his growth and progress. "Samuel grew, and the Lord was with him, and did let none of his words fall to the ground" (verse 19). Not only did this prove to be true, but the climactic moment in the boy's experience swiftly became known throughout all the land. "All Israel from Dan even to Beer-sheba knew that Samuel was established to be a prophet of the Lord" (verse 20).

Samuel: Reformer, Judge, and Priest

Samuel, who from childhood had been trained in the temple and was hailed as a prophet at an early age, was not yet in his teens when the Lord revealed to him the approaching doom of the sons of Eli the priest, Hophni and Phinehas, whose activities had demeaned the sacred office of priesthood (see I Sam. 3:13).

Israel had unwisely become involved in battle with the Philistines, and in the opening skirmish four thousand of the Hebrew warriors were slain. Stunned by this unforeseen reverse, the elders of Israel, evidently with the connivance of Eli's sons, brought the sacred "ark of the covenant" into their camp, confident that this rash act would assure them of victory. Actually it spurred the Philistines to stronger efforts against them. The Israelites were routed, Hophni and Phinehas were slain, and the ark itself was captured (see I Sam. 4:1–11).

It is not until some twenty years later that we again hear directly of Samuel and his activities. It is natural, however, to assume that during these years Samuel was continuing to prepare himself for his great mission and that his fame and influence gradually increased until he became convinced that the time had come for him to raise the standard of reformation. So he who in his younger days had been hailed as a prophet now appears as a reformer.

Despite the lessons Israel might well have learned from the unexpected victory of the Philistines twenty years before, and from the capture of their sacred ark, which symbolized the presence and protection of the one true God, they still compromised with idolatry. But Samuel's patient work had not been in vain, for when he now called upon his nation to renounce idols representing the Canaanite deity Baal and images of the so-called goddess Asherah, his appeal was heard. "The children of Israel did put away Baalim and Ashtaroth, and served the Lord only" (I Sam. 7:4).

Here is abundant proof of the great influence wielded by Samuel. For many years his countrymen had been in bondage to idolatry. Now, at his stirring call, they were prepared to make a definite break from it. What further encouraged them in taking this forward step was his assurance that God Himself would deliver them "out of the hand of the Philistines" (verse 3).

To establish and confirm the promise of the Israelites, Samuel now called for a national gathering at Mizpah, where he would pray for them. At this gathering they fasted and confessed their sins, while Samuel proceeded to judge them, a task which continued throughout his life (see verse 15).

At this point a further challenge to their growing faith presented itself. The Philistines, noting the great concourse of people gathered at Mizpah, prepared to advance against them. Fear swept over the Israelites, who urged the continuance of Samuel's prayers on their behalf.

Without delay Samuel undertook yet another of his numerous offices, acting on this occasion as a priest. As he offered a burnt offering to the Lord, the Philistines advanced. But they were discouraged by ominous peals of thunder, while the Israelites, now confident of their success, drove their enemies back to Beth-car, probably on the borders of Philistia. In commemoration of this signal victory, Samuel erected a great stone near Mizpah, naming it Ebenezer (literally "stone of help") and stressing its significance in the words: "Hitherto hath the Lord helped us" (verse 12).

CHAPTER IV ·

The Development of Kingship

Monarchy in Israel: Part I

The defeat of a Philistine army at Ebenezer (see I Sam. 7:10–13) seems to have held the Philistine forces in check for some time, thus upholding Samuel's position as leader of the Israelites. However, in his later years, while retaining his own judgeship, he appointed his two sons to share his responsibilities, stationing them in the southern frontier town of Beersheba. This was an unwise choice, for they "took bribes, and perverted judgment," leading "the elders of Israel" to demand their replacement by one whom they termed "a king to judge us like all the nations" (8:3–5).

It is generally conceded that I Samuel contains at least two interwoven but widely variant accounts of Saul's appointment as Israel's first king. One of these early writers considers this as a normal development from judgeship to monarchy, demanded by the people and their elders, and in accord with the growing status of Israel as a strongly integrated national group.

However, another, and probably a later, writer views the rise of kingship as a bold denial of the sole leadership of Israel's God. The earlier source, then, considers monarchy as a practical and progressive step, in no way conflicting with the overall government of Deity. The later record, perhaps more ecclesiastical in its approach, pleads for God's exclusive rule, without trace or taint of human government.

Thus in Chapter 9, one of the passages strongly upholding and approving Samuel's sponsorship of Saul, this young Benjamite, the son of Kish, is introduced as both handsome and of commanding height. Moreover, it is recorded that Saul was approved by the Lord Himself, "And when Samuel saw Saul, the Lord said unto him, Behold the man whom I spake to thee of! this same shall reign over my people" (verse 17).

In the following chapter significant omens appear, stressing the deep interest shown in Saul by the aged prophet, together with Samuel's strict obedience to the plans and promises which he understood to await this promising young man, who was not yet completely aware of his royal destiny.

True, the prophet had already assured Saul that "the desire of Israel" — presumably the fervent hopes and desires of the nation — rested upon him and his family. Saul had wondered how this could possibly be, since Benjamin was the smallest of the tribes and his own family the least within its borders (see verses 20, 21).

But God's plan for Saul, as Samuel envisioned it, was not to be denied, and he anointed the young man in God's name "to be captain over his inheritance" (10:1). Samuel also promised that the traditional sign of divine approval — "the Spirit of the Lord," — would come upon him, enabling him to share in the work of prophecy — a proceeding which was to change his very nature (see verse 6).

Later, Saul's prompt deliverance of the town of Jabesh-gilead from an attack by the Ammonites awakened the Israelites to the potentialities of his generalship (see 11:1–11). At Samuel's suggestion they confirmed his secret anointing of Saul at God's command, "And all the people went to Gilgal; and there they made Saul king before the Lord in Gilgal" (verse 15).

This outlines the earlier account of how Saul came to be king; representing him as chosen by God, anointed by Samuel, and finally gladly accepted by his subjects. The later and alternative interpretation follows.

Monarchy in Israel: Part II

As noted previously, the venal and irresponsible acts of Samuel's sons, whom he had appointed as judges, led to a demand that the position of judge be abolished forthwith and be replaced by a monarchical government.

One of the historians who writes in the First Book of Samuel represents the Lord as concurring with Samuel in wholeheartedly agreeing with this plan, as we have shown. However, an alternative account, now to be considered, gives a strikingly different interpretation of the situation. The actions and demands of the people and their elders, this later writer contended, disobeyed God's commands and ignored His righteous government, rebelling against Him and His loyal prophet Samuel.

Traces of this second account, closely intertwined with the earlier one by later editing, soon begin to appear (see I Sam. 8:5, 6). Instead of accepting the elders' plan, the prophet expresses displeasure; and when he turns to God for advice, he receives an ominous response. He is to give consideration to the people's plea, but, the divine message continues, "they have not rejected thee, but they have rejected me, that I should not reign over them" (verse 7).

As Chapter 8 continues, the Lord reminds the prophet of the manner in which the people have forsaken Him to serve pagan deities. Samuel is to give them a king if they insist upon it, but he must warn them of what such a step will involve. No longer will they be free men but virtually serfs. The best of their lands and of their crops will be confiscated by royal decree. But even when Samuel announces to them the impending consequences of the course they have chosen, they refuse to listen.

In Chapter 10, verse 17, the prophet is said to have "called the people together unto the Lord," to Mizpah, the very place where they had routed the Philistines with God's help (see 7:10, 11). But on this occasion Samuel again reminds Israel of how they have rejected their God by virtually demanding a king in His place. Whereas in the earlier account of Saul's elevation to the throne both Samuel and the Lord had been represented as choosing and accepting him gladly, now he is selected primarily by the device of casting lots (see 10:19–22). Heedless of the pitfalls of monarchy of which they had been warned, "all the people shouted, and said, God save the king" (verse 24).

In Chapter 12 Samuel, in a dignified farewell speech, turns over his authority to the ruler whom the people had demanded. While reminding them of the wrong they have committed against him and against his God, Samuel nobly agrees to pray for them and to continue to teach them "the good and the right way" (verse 23).

In reviewing these varying and in some respects conflicting

accounts of the elevation of Saul to the throne as the first Hebrew king, we may consider that they simply represent differing aspects of the same historical situation. Doubtless the Israelites required strong leadership to hold the position of a relatively minor state, largely surrounded by hostile pagan tribes. Still they had to be reminded not to forget the leadership provided by their God and by staunch representatives of His higher power, such as Samuel. In advancing politically, they could not afford to neglect the moral and spiritual guidance on which their nation was founded and which alone could assure their continued success.

Saul the Wayward King

Following his accession to the throne of Israel, Saul collected three thousand men, forming the nucleus of an army for the impending struggle with the Philistines. Actually it was his son Jonathan who precipitated the fray by attacking a Philistine garrison; and to support him, Saul called his subjects to arms, anticipating their loyal response. The result was discouraging. Many, terrorized by the vastly superior forces of their enemies, fled eastward to Gilead; others hid in caves and empty wells. Such as rallied to Saul's standard "followed him trembling" (see I Sam. 13:1–7).

To evaluate the events which followed, one may recall that when Samuel anointed Saul as king, he insisted that Saul marshal his forces at Gilgal and await the coming of the prophet, who would offer sacrifices to God. "Seven days shalt thou tarry, till I come to thee, and shew thee what thou shalt do" (I Sam. 10:8).

Saul had now encamped at Gilgal as instructed, but as day after day passed, the Philistine opposition appeared increasingly menacing. His men were deserting him, and he could see no sign of Samuel; so Saul took matters into his own hands, offering sacrifice independently, apparently on the seventh day. At this point Samuel appeared and denounced Saul's action. While Saul had obeyed the letter of the law, he had ignored the spirit of the instructions he had received. In self-willed insistence on his personal planning Saul had forfeited his kingdom (see I Sam. 13:8–13).

True, he was permitted to retain it until his demise, but it would not pass to his son; indeed Samuel informed Saul that God had already selected his successor. "The Lord hath sought him a man after his own heart" (verse 14) — or, as it can also be translated, "a man in accord with his mind" — in contrast to Saul who was prone to act upon his own judgment.

Thus rejected and thrown back on his own resources, Saul soon found that now but six hundred men followed him; and even when he joined forces with Jonathan's contingent, it was to discover that only he and his son were adequately armed (see verses 19–22). However a brave and surprisingly successful individual attack on a Philistine outpost by Jonathan and his armor-bearer not only slew a score of their foes but spread panic among the Philistine host (see I Sam. 14:1, 6–16).

At last the Israelites were gaining the upper hand; but their success was marred by an ill-considered oath which Saul had enjoined upon them — that they should eat nothing all day on pain of death. They became so weak from hunger that they could not follow up their advantage, and many of their foes escaped. Even Jonathan, who had been absent when the oath was exacted, inadvertently violated it by eating wild honey, and would have been slain by his father, had not Saul's soldiers pled for his life, insisting that Jonathan had "wrought with God this day" (verse 45).

Further evidence of the waywardness and disobedience which contributed to Saul's downfall is seen in his failure to destroy utterly the Amalekites and their stock, in obedience to what was considered to be a divine command (see I Sam. 15). Saul offered the excuse that he had saved the best of the animals to offer them to the Lord, but he was reminded by Samuel that "to obey is better than sacrifice" (verse 22), and that the humility of his earlier days should not have been displaced by pride.

CHAPTER V ·

The Career of David

David the Shepherd Lad

The prophet Samuel had held high hopes for the success of King Saul; and now after Saul's disobedience (see I Sam. 15) bemoaned his downfall. But the Lord Himself indicated, the account tells us, that this was no time for tears. Rather Samuel should take steps to anoint a new king, whom he was to select from among the eight sons of Jesse, the Bethlehemite. Jesse's farm was situated some five miles south of the modern Jerusalem.

Fully aware of the jealous disposition of Saul, the prophet hesitated to make any overtures toward one who might be destined to claim Saul's royal estate, but he was told that while he was performing a sacrifice at Bethlehem God would reveal to him the identity of the new ruler.

Seven of Jesse's sons passed before Samuel in quick succession, until at last the youngest, David, was called from his sheep at the prophet's insistence. He was a stalwart young man, described as ruddy, beautiful, and "goodly to look to" (I Sam. 16:12). His selection was quickly confirmed by the

Lord, the old account tells us, in the words: "Arise, anoint him: for this is he." So Samuel anointed the lad and "the Spirit of the Lord came upon David from that day forward" (verse 13).

David's father, Jesse, was a member of the noted tribe of Judah, the grandson of those well-known characters, Boaz and Ruth. But the young shepherd seems neither to have heeded his heritage nor perhaps even his future destiny. He returned quietly to tend his father's flocks, until he was called to soothe the malady of Saul, whom he was later to succeed.

It is evident from the Biblical record that King Saul had become subject to intermittent attacks of mental derangement. In seeking to calm their master in such periods of stress, his servants prescribed the services of an expert player of the harp, who might bring him solace and healing. They commended to his special attention David, the son of Jesse, noting that he was an accomplished musician, a handsome young man, an active and successful warrior, and also a man well prepared to feel and practice the presence of God (see verse 18).

Saul at once sent messengers to Jesse, calling for his talented son. The king's request was promptly granted; and when David reached the palace, he was graciously and gratefully accepted. We read of King Saul that "he loved him greatly; and he became his armourbearer" (verse 21), a position of special trust and honor in Bible times. Not only so; but when Saul's malady troubled him, David's music had its desired effect, for "Saul was refreshed, and was well, and the evil spirit departed from him" (verse 23).

In the following chapter we read that the Philistine forces again attacked Israel, taking their position on a hill some fourteen miles west of Bethlehem, separated from Saul's men by a deep valley. This was the memorable occasion on which the young David won the gratitude of Israel by boldly accepting the giant Goliath's challenge to single combat when Saul's men were panic-stricken. Although the giant has been estimated at some nine and one half feet in height, according to data given in this account, with armor and weapons in proportion, David slew him by the expert use of his shepherd's sling. This brave act broke the morale of the Philistine host and presaged the many future exploits which were to be associated with David's name.

David and Jonathan

David and Jonathan shared a friendship still proverbial for its beauty, strength, and permanence. Apparently they first met following David's triumphant mastery over Goliath, proved on the basis that "the battle is the Lord's" (I Sam. 17:47); and a mutually irresistible attraction quickly arose between them. "The soul of Jonathan was knit with the soul of David, and Jonathan loved him as his own soul" (18:1).

It says much for their inherent stability and loyalty that never in the ensuing years of stress did they violate this covenant.

At first, Jonathan's father, Saul, did not hesitate to place David in charge of a band of warriors, but soon bitter jealousy assailed him on learning that David was credited with destroying tens of thousands of his country's foes, and Saul mere thousands (see 18:8).

Later Saul allowed David to marry his daughter Michal, although with a sinister purpose, "that she may be a snare to him" (verse 21). "Saul became David's enemy continually" (verse 29). He insisted that even Jonathan must join his retainers in killing David.

Here was a severe test of Jonathan's love for his friend; but he met that test. He pled so urgently with Saul that for the present his counsel prevailed and Saul swore by a solemn oath that David should be spared (see 19:6). Later he reversed his own decision by again seeking to transfix him with a javelin, as he had before the reconciliation (see 18:11; 19:10).

Following a moving renewal of their love and loyalty toward one another, David and Jonathan apparently reached the reluctant conclusion that David must flee into the wild hilly areas of southern Palestine to escape Saul's wrath (see 20:41, 42).

At a later date Jonathan, unknown to his vengeful father, sought out David in a wooded section in the wilderness of Ziph, some miles to the south of Hebron, providing all the help and encouragement of which he was capable, for he "strengthened his hand in God" (23:16).

Jonathan assured his friend that Saul would never find him, in spite of all his efforts. Moreover David could be certain that he would indeed rule over Israel and that Jonathan would stand shoulder to shoulder with him, as Saul was well aware. On this occasion the two friends once again entered into a solemn agreement "before the Lord," reconfirming the pact which they had sworn to obey (verse 18). As far as the record goes, they never met again, but David never forgot his faithful friend.

It seems that when David next heard of his beloved Jonathan, it was to receive the sad news that both he and his father Saul had been slain in battle. For all his faults, Saul had been king of Israel, and David included him and his son in a noble epitaph: "Saul and Jonathan were lovely and pleasant in their lives, and in their death they were not divided"; while to Jonathan he paid a more personal tribute: "Very pleasant hast thou been unto me: thy love to me was wonderful, passing the love of women" (II Sam. 1:23, 26).

Later still, when David himself ascended the throne of Israel, he quieted the fears of Jonathan's son Mephibosheth. He invited him to be a perpetual guest at the royal table, and assured his tenure of his inheritance as grandson of Saul, and the son of Jonathan, David's closest friend (see II Sam. 9).

David's Growing Leadership

During the concluding years of Saul's reign, his enmity toward David had become increasingly bitter. Hence the son of Jesse fled into the wilderness, gathering around him at the cave of Adullam, near the borders of Philistia, a band of men who had been forced to live the life of outlaws. He soon appeared as undisputed leader of four hundred staunch supporters (see I Sam. 22:1, 2).

As his defiance of the reigning monarch put his family at Bethlehem in a dangerous position, he placed his parents under the protection of the king of Moab, a wise step and a logical one, in view of the fact that his great grandmother, Ruth, was a Moabitess (see verses 3, 4).

Various aspects of David's experiences in the wilderness throw light upon his character. Although Saul was making every effort to arrest him, David ignored his personal danger, going promptly and boldly to the aid of his friends at Keilah, a Judean town now facing a savage attack by the Philistines.

David's courage and leadership of his men turned the tide of battle in favor of Keilah, and the Philistines were defeated (see 23:1–5).

David had little difficulty in eluding Saul amid the hills of the Judean countryside, which were familiar to him from his experience as a shepherd. But the fact that David had now entered Keilah to protect and save its inhabitants was regarded by Saul, not as an errand of mercy to aid Saul's own subjects, but as an opportunity for slaying his rival. Saul was prepared to dispatch an army to besiege and capture Keilah, and especially David and his followers. Learning of this plan, David turned to God in his extremity; and he and his men, now numbering some six hundred, escaped again to their mountain strongholds (see verses 7–14).

Saul's forces continued to make every effort to surround David and his band. They seemed to be on the point of fulfilling their purpose when David was saved once again, for Saul received an urgent message to protect his country from an unexpected Philistine invasion (see verses 26, 27).

Chapter 24 of I Samuel casts further light upon David's generosity toward Saul. Unaware of David's presence, Saul entered a cave in which the fugitive was hiding. Here, surely, was David's opportunity to slay his rival, but he refused even to touch him. However, as proof of his presence he cut off a portion of Saul's royal robe. Later he showed this to the king as evidence of the fact that he had no desire to harm him. Momentarily Saul repented, tearfully crying out: "Is this thy voice, my son David?" (verse 16.)

What is apparently an alternative account appears in a later passage (see Chapter 26), where David is said to have approached Saul, surrounded by his followers, as all slept soundly. According to this record, David carried off the jar of water standing by Saul's head, and also the great spear, symbolic of royal authority, which was planted in the ground beside him. When later David shouted across the valley to the startled ruler, Saul said, as before, "Is this thy voice, my son David?" adding the words of penitence: "I have sinned: return, my son David . . ." (verses 17, 21).

David's response is significant: "The Lord delivered thee into my hand to day, but I would not stretch forth mine hand against the Lord's anointed" (verse 23).

David the Psalmist

David's name is so closely associated with the book of Psalms that we may well consider his relationship to these familiar and beautiful poems. As printed in the King James Version of the Bible, they appear to be in prose; but many more recent translators set them down in metrical form.

While more than seventy of the one hundred and fifty psalms are described as psalms "of David," especially in the headings preceding many of the poems, the Hebrew phrase *le Dawid* can as literally be rendered either "to David" or "for David." This suggests that some, at least, were not composed by David himself but were dedicated to him. Some of the psalms, indeed, presuppose historical situations earlier than David's day. Others clearly refer to events occurring long after his time.

The writer of II Samuel in reporting "the last words of David" (23:1), describes him as the "sweet psalmist of Israel" — the most famous poet in Jewish national history. The rabbis even went so far as to ascribe *all* the psalms to him. It may well be that we do owe to this poet-king the nucleus of this inspiring collection of early Hebrew hymns. Yet many authors, named or unnamed, seem to have contributed to the collection, as occurs in the compilation of hymnals in our own time, many of which still draw upon the Biblical Psalter.

Many of these poems are connected, according to their introductory headings, with actual events in David's life. Thus Psalm 3 is said to have been composed by him when he was forced to flee before his own son, Absalom, who sought to usurp David's throne (see II Sam. 15:14). Even in these physical and emotional straits, it appears, the king claimed that "salvation belongeth unto the Lord" (Ps. 3:8). Equally vivid is the background of Psalm 63, said to have been written when David "was in the wilderness of Judah," which is still largely "a dry and thirsty land, where no water is" (verse 1). And the repeated divine deliverances which came to him as he sought to escape the jealous wrath of his predecessor Saul might have inspired him to compose the eighteenth Psalm.

Another great leader traditionally associated with the composition of the book of Psalms, was Moses, who lived several centuries before the reign of David, and was said to have contributed to this collection "a prayer of Moses the man of God," found in Psalm 90. It includes this inspired assurance: "Lord, thou hast been our dwelling place in all generations," and the reminder that "from everlasting to everlasting, thou art God" (verses 1 and 2).

Some dozen psalms are attributed to a Levite named Asaph or his family (Ps. 50 and 73–83), who apparently had part in the music and song of the temple. (See I Chron. 15:16–19; 25:1–9.)

From the time of the captivity of the Jews in Babylon, in the sixth and fifth centuries B.C., long after David's day, must surely date Psalm 137. "How shall we sing the Lord's song in a strange land?" cried the exiles, telling how "by the rivers of Babylon, there we sat down, yea, we wept, when we remembered Zion" (verses 4 and 1).

The extent of David's personal contributions to the psalms may never be known, but Christ Jesus himself, so often hailed as "the Son of David" (for example in Matt. 21:9), had no hesitation in quoting from them repeatedly. Thus we, too, as followers of the Master, owe much to that "sweet psalmist of Israel."

David the King

With the passing of Saul and Jonathan in battle, the kingship devolved upon David as Samuel had foretold. As a result of prayer he proceeded to Hebron, where he was anointed "king over the house of Judah" by the Judeans themselves, reigning there for "seven years and six months" (II Sam. 2:4, 11).

David's rule, however, was by no means undisputed. Saul's supporters had crowned his son Ish-bosheth as king in the territory of Gilead to the east of the Jordan, with influence extending "over Ephraim, and over Benjamin, and over all Israel" (verse 9). Here, then, were the elements of civil war, but there could be no doubt concerning the eventual outcome of the strife between the two kings, for "David waxed stronger and stronger, and the house of Saul waxed weaker and weaker" (3:1) until, at the age of thirty-seven, David was accepted as monarch of a united kingdom of Judah and all Israel combined (see 5:1–5).

It was apparently about this time that Jerusalem became the capital of the Hebrew nation. Taking its central fortress of Zion by storm, David renamed the town "the city of David" in honor of this event and established his court there (see I Chron. 11:4–7). Since Jerusalem lay almost on the boundary between the tribal territory of Judah and that of Benjamin, the selection of this city for David's capital was a wise one, calculated to satisfy both the members of David's own tribe of Judah, and those who, like Saul, were Benjamites. David also transferred the sacred "ark of the covenant" to Jerusalem, thus identifying the city as a religious center (see II Sam. 6).

In fact the pomp now associated with David's personal residence led the king to propose the erection of a stately temple for the housing of the ark, which hitherto had been kept in a humble tabernacle or tent. The Lord commended the plan, the Bible account tells us, through the instrumentality of Nathan the prophet. But David was informed that not by himself but by his famous son whom we know as Solomon would the temple eventually be erected. He received the promise that his throne would be "established for ever" (II Sam. 7:16).

David's success in the wars he waged in furthering the advancement of his kingdom is unquestioned, but his personal and domestic affairs were sometimes less fortunate or praiseworthy. In his desire to make Bath-sheba his queen, David arranged that her husband, Uriah, should be left unsupported while leading an assault against an Ammonite stronghold. When Uriah was slain, as David had anticipated, Bath-sheba "became his wife, and bare him a son. But the thing that David had done displeased the Lord" (11:27).

Nathan the prophet rebuked David with a parable. He told the story of "one little ewe lamb," cherished by a poor man but wantonly killed by his wealthy neighbor to provide food for an unexpected guest. Incensed at the injustice, David cried that such a man should surely die, only to hear Nathan's stern response, "Thou art the man" (12:7). Because of his prompt and sincere repentance, the king's own life was spared, although his first child by Bath-sheba did not survive. Later, however, Bath-sheba became the mother of Solomon, David's successor.

David's Later Years

As David's reign proceeded and his power increased, he organized a more elaborate system of government than had existed before his time, selecting a "cabinet" to aid him in his administration of Israel's affairs (see II Sam. 8:16–18).

Joab, who had already proved himself to be a skillful general, was placed in charge of military affairs, while Benaiah was appointed as captain of the royal guard. A certain Jehoshaphat was chosen as "recorder," which may well imply that he acted as official historiographer. Religious affairs were in no way neglected, for Zadok and Ahimelech are listed as "the priests." Other officials included Ahithophel, "David's counsellor," and "Hushai, David's friend" (15:12, 37), presumably confidential advisers to the king.

Assured of the Lord's protection and support, David made every effort to execute "judgment and justice unto all his people" (8:15). In planning for the future development and continuity of his kingdom, he appointed his sons as "chief rulers" (verse 18).

Logical as such a step might appear to be, we gather that the king himself, for all his success as an executive, had shown a surprising lack of firmness where his children were concerned, especially in his dealings with his handsome son Adonijah. In fact, he had allowed this young man, as he grew up, to do whatever he chose, without making any effort to train or rebuke him. "His father," we read, "had not displeased him at any time in saying, Why hast thou done so?" (I Kings 1:6.) Indeed Adonijah's elder brother, Absalom, also showed the bitter results of their father's lack of discipline.

It was then toward the close of David's reign that he was shocked by the treachery shown by his favorite son Absalom, who sought to undermine the loyalty of his father's subjects and to seize the kingdom for himself. Absalom's persistent claim was that if only he were accepted as ruler of the land he would show a constant fairness and justice to all, which, he insinuated, David lacked. The result was that, as the Bible vividly puts it, "Absalom stole the hearts of the men of Israel" (II Sam. 15:6).

In the face of this insidious and unforeseen rebellion, David was forced to abandon his capital, taking with him in his flight his staunch supporters. But it is typical of his continued faith that he left the priests and the "ark of the covenant" in Jerusalem, clearly trusting in God's will for him, and not thinking to get aid from this sacred symbol of divine authority (see 15:24–26). His confidence was justified, for the rebellion soon collapsed. Absalom himself, to his father's deep sorrow, was slain in battle. Thus the way was opened for David's return to power.

When David foresaw that his long years of service to his country might be nearing their conclusion, he took steps to establish the succession of Bath-sheba's son Solomon to his throne. But before David's plans could be put into effect,

Adonijah put in his personal claim, and many recognized it, calling him "king Adonijah" (see I Kings 1:5–25). At this David showed a sudden return of his old fire and had Solomon anointed forthwith as his successor. The cry rang out, "God save king Solomon" (verse 34), while the claims and pretensions of Adonijah faded even more swiftly than had those of Absalom.

CHAPTER VI ·

The Power of Solomon

Solomon: Builder of the Temple

While Bath-sheba's first child by David had passed on in infancy, she later bore him other sons, of whom the most famed was Solomon. Raised in the royal palace, he must have observed his father's skillful handling of many trying situations assailing him during his later years — rebellion, treachery, and civil war. Thus when Solomon became king, he had already been trained in the school of experience. We read in I Kings 2:12, "Then sat Solomon upon the throne of David his father; and his kingdom was established greatly."

David was a warrior king; but Solomon, whose very name implies peace, seems to have turned his attention to the maintenance of his realm and to a wide program of building, including various royal residences, cities and walls for national defense (see I Kings 7:1–12; 9:15–19).

But of all Solomon's projects, the most famous was the temple at Jerusalem, planned by David but deferred by God's direction to the less warlike reign of his son. David had amassed quantities of building materials for use when the work actually began: hewn stones for the walls, cedar lumber in abundance, brass hinges and iron nails (see I Chron. 22:1–6).

Solomon enlisted the aid of Hiram, king of Tyre, the most noted contractor of the day, to supervise the project, providing skilled artisans and any additional materials needed to complete it. After about three years the work began in earnest. The temple was a relatively small edifice, for its interior measurements have been estimated at ninety feet in length, thirty broad, and forty-five in height. Its walls were of stone and of great thickness. It was paneled on the inside with cedar, largely overlaid with gold. According to I Kings 6:38 it took seven years to build. It was erected on Mount Moriah (see II Chron. 3:1), generally identified with Mount Zion; and parts of its retaining walls still exist, made up of stones so massive that they are estimated to weigh some hundred tons apiece.

In spite of the beauty and stability of the temple, its religious significance was of far deeper moment, as Solomon made plain at its dedication, vividly described in II Chronicles (Chapters 5, 6, and 7).

Innumerable sacrifices of sheep and oxen were offered, symbolizing the people's gifts to God and the offering of themselves to His service; and as the sacred ark was placed in the special sanctuary prepared for it, the priests and Levites joined in a song of praise set to instrumental music. "The glory of the Lord had filled the house of God" (5:14).

Chapter 6 describes Solomon's part in this ceremony. He began by blessing the assembled throng, reminding them of how his father had planned to build this temple and how he himself had now completed it in accord with God's will. Instead of following the ancient custom of standing at prayer, the king now humbly "kneeled down upon his knees" (verse 13), and instead of boasting of the grandeur of this shrine, he cried (verse 18): "Behold, heaven and the heaven of heavens cannot contain thee; how much less this house which I have built!" As he rose from his knees, according to II Chronicles, there came the sign of divine approval (7:1): "Fire came down from heaven, and consumed the burnt offering and the sacrifices." The balance of the chapter shows that the continuance of such divine favor depended not merely on the number of material offerings but on obedience to God's will.

Solomon's Wisdom

Famous as Solomon was for his great building program, his desire for wisdom was perhaps more typical of him. Early in his reign he had a God-given opportunity to further this desire. He had already shown evidence of his love for the Lord and his obedience to the statutes promulgated by his father, David. Now at the sanctuary of Gibeon he saw the Lord appear to him in a dream and proclaim, "Ask what I shall give thee" (I Kings 3:5).

Before making his request, Solomon proved his humility and his preparedness for the great gifts awaiting him. He expressed deep gratitude for the divine goodness and protection shown him and his royal father. As far as he was concerned, he felt little more than an infant in the handling of the wide domain he had inherited.

"I am but a little child," he cried, in the vein of Moses before him (see Ex. 3:11) and of Jeremiah at a later date (see Jer. 1:6). "I know not how to go out or come in. . . . Give therefore thy servant an understanding heart to judge thy people, that I may discern between good and bad" (I Kings 3:7–9). His plea was abundantly granted. Not only did he receive a wise and understanding heart but also honor and riches, which he had not requested.

Before long, the ancient record continues, the king was able to prove his sagacity. Two women came before him for judgment, each carrying an infant — one alive and one not — and each claiming to be the mother of the living child. When Solomon suggested that the child should be cut in half and thus be divided equally between them, one woman callously agreed. The other identified herself as the true parent by her readiness to renounce the infant rather than witness its execution (see verses 16–27).

The Bible records that news of this astute decision spread apace and Solomon became noted for his wide practice of wisdom, exceeding that "of all the children of the east country" (4:30), famed for their own sagacity.

There appears to be little to indicate that Solomon's wisdom was of a strictly spiritual character. His astuteness and business acumen were unquestionably remarkable, but his later life was soon to show that much of his success was at the expense of that "pure religion and undefiled before God," praised in the New Testament (James 1:27).

The most famous of Solomon's numerous visitors was the queen of Sheba, who traveled in state from a distant country to meet this monarch of whose wealth and wisdom she had heard so much and who came with the avowed intention of testing him "with hard questions" (I Kings 10:1).

Tradition vies with legend in suggesting the nature of these questions, although it is implied that he answered them so satisfactorily that the queen had no hesitation in admitting to

Solomon that "the half was not told me: thy wisdom and prosperity exceedeth the fame which I heard" (verse 7).

The exact position of the queen's own kingdom is uncertain, although its general area is suggested in the New Testament, where she is described as "the queen of the south" (Matt. 12:42). This might well indicate that she held her court somewhere in the broad area of Arabia to the east of the Red Sea.

A persistent tradition upheld by the present royal dynasty of Ethiopia associates the queen with that land, claiming for the kings of Ethiopia direct descent from Solomon and the queen of Sheba.

Solomon in All His Glory

Further aspects of Solomon's career deserve our consideration, contributing as they do to the brilliance of his reign but also to its limitations.

His literary efforts were numerous and varied. Like David, he was famed as a poet; he was credited with more than a thousand songs (see I Kings 4:32). Tradition ascribed to him the famed "Song of Songs," implying in Hebrew idiom, "the most beautiful of songs." While having no direct reference to Deity — though it has been allegorically interpreted, as the headings of the King James Version indicate — it contains much of beauty and charm, vividly describing the birds, flowers, trees, and vineyards of Israel, welcoming the close of winter and the advance of spring (see S. of Sol. 2:11, 12). Emphasis is laid upon a country maiden and her peasant lover, to whom she remains true in spite of her royal suitor. The poet cries, "Many waters cannot quench love" (8:7).

Solomon appears to have been equally noted for his proverbs, three thousand of which are assigned to him (see I Kings 4:32). Passages in the book of Proverbs do contain references to "the proverbs of Solomon," but other contributors are also mentioned. It seems clear that just as tradition attributed all, or almost all, psalms to David — although some may have been earlier, and many clearly later than David's time — so Solomon was viewed as the typical writer of proverbs. His reputed authorship of the book of Ecclesiastes is not generally accepted today, but he is thought to have composed a book or books dealing with natural history. He wrote of trees and plants from the lofty cedar of Lebanon down to the lowly hyssop "that springeth out of the wall" (I Kings 4:33); also animals, birds, fish, and reptiles.

The immense wealth amassed by Solomon came to him largely through foreign trade, for he seems to have maintained a fleet of ships at Ezion-geber, near Eloth on the Gulf of Aqaba. These ships sailed repeatedly to and from Ophir, identified by some with India and well known as a rich source of gold (see I Kings 9:26–28).

Others of Solomon's ships sailed westward through the Mediterranean to Tarshish, probably on the coast of Spain (see II Chron. 9:21). The king's foreign trade by land was doubtless mainly with Hiram, king of Tyre, and with the rulers of Egypt.

In his dealings with the queen of Sheba, Solomon stood at the peak of his riches and success. But soon the flaws in his prosperity became apparent. In his later years he largely forgot the high ideals of humility and the strict obedience to God's will that he had set himself early in his reign.

In Exodus 34:16, the chosen people had been commanded never to marry women from pagan tribes or countries. Yet in flagrant disobedience Solomon himself married not only Pharaoh's daughter but some seven hundred other princesses, and "his wives turned away his heart after other gods" (I Kings 11:4). Retribution came swiftly; for when he passed away his own son, Rehoboam, lost most of his father's empire, retaining Judah alone.

Later, Christ Jesus could refer to "Solomon in all his glory" (Matt. 6:29), noting that all the magnificence of Solomon could not compare with the beauty of the wild flowers of Galilee. Indeed Jesus knew, "Ye cannot serve God and mammon" (verse 24), or, as Goodspeed translates, "You cannot serve God and money."

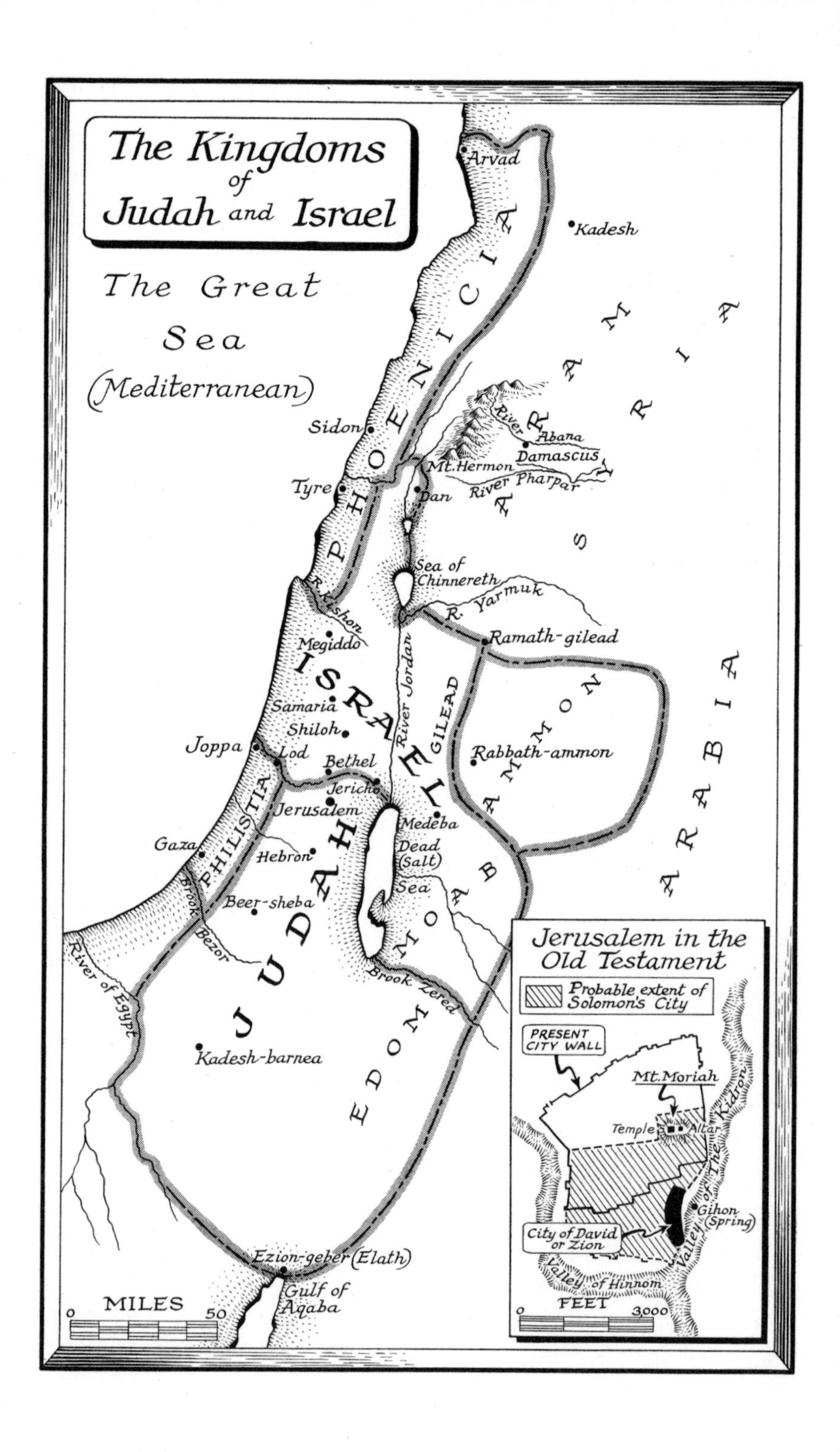
The Kingdoms of Judah and Israel
The Great Sea (Mediterranean)
Arvad
Kadesh
PHOENICIA
ARAM
SYRIA
Sidon
River Abana
Damascus
Mt. Hermon
Tyre
River Pharpar
Dan
Sea of Chinnereth
R. Yarmuk
Megiddo
Ramath-gilead
ISRAEL
Samaria
Shiloh
River Jordan
GILEAD
AMMON
ARABIA
Joppa
Lod
Bethel
Rabbath-ammon
Jericho
PHILISTIA
Jerusalem
Medeba
Gaza
Hebron
Dead (Salt) Sea
MOAB
Beer-sheba
Brook Bezor
River of Egypt
Brook Zered
JUDAH
Kadesh-barnea
EDOM
Ezion-geber (Elath)
Gulf of Aqaba
MILES
0
50
Jerusalem in the Old Testament
Probable extent of Solomon's City
PRESENT CITY WALL
Mt. Moriah
Temple
Altar
Valley of the Kidron
Gihon (Spring)
City of David or Zion
Valley of Hinnom
FEET
0
3000

CHAPTER VII ·

The Rise of Oral Prophecy

Monarchy Bows Before Prophecy

At the close of Solomon's reign it must surely have become evident to the people that the ominous prediction of Samuel (see I Sam. 8:18) concerning the dangers and limitations often inherent in human kingship had been all too accurate. It is true that monarchy had had every opportunity to prove its value. Even Saul, in spite of his self-will and his moody and vengeful character, possessed the potentialities of greatness. David and Solomon were undoubtedly great in many respects, but we are faced by a national record marred by discord and idolatry when Solomon passed away.

The united kingdom of Israel, established by David and raised by Solomon to the status of an empire, noted for its wide commercial enterprises and material wealth, now came to an abrupt end. It was replaced by two minor, separate kingdoms, Judah in the south and Israel — in the geographical sense of the term — in the northern part of Palestine.

On Solomon's passing, then, his son Rehoboam claimed the right to succeed him; but when the people agreed to serve him on one condition, that he would lighten "the grievous service" and "heavy yoke" his father had laid upon them, he spurned their request, making the arbitrary statement, "My father hath chastised you with whips, but I will chastise you with scorpions" (I Kings 12:4, 11), possibly referring to increased taxation.

Not unnaturally, the response to such obstinacy was rebellion; and while Rehoboam ruled at Jerusalem in Judah, the northern province of Israel with its ten tribes was seized by Jeroboam, whom Solomon had once sought to slay (see 11:40), clearly anticipating such a traitorous move.

This political cleavage between north and south caused an even more serious religious division. Jeroboam erected two golden images in the form of calves, one at Dan in the north, the other at Bethel in the south of his kingdom (see 12:28–30), to discourage his subjects from visiting the temple of the Lord at Jerusalem, the capital of his rival, thus encouraging idolatry.

The moral and spiritual causes underlying the downfall of Solomon's empire are readily apparent. Both he and David had commenced their reigns with strong trust in the true God of Israel as their support and guide in all their endeavors. David had planned for and Solomon had completed a great temple in honor of Israel's God. But Solomon had no hesitation in erecting temples to heathen deities worshiped by his almost innumerable pagan wives.

David's unfortunate union with Bath-sheba had already contributed to the lack of moral standards indicated in his son's matrimonial affairs; and this disintegration in normal family life could hardly fail to break down the moral fiber of their subjects. Moreover, Solomon's undue emphasis in his later years on material rather than on spiritual riches must have contributed to the collapse of his proud empire.

For half a century following Solomon's demise, unrest, confusion, and idolatry were rife in both Judah and Israel; and during this period we read the ominous reminder that ruler after ruler "did evil in the sight of the Lord" (15:26, 34; 16:30).

More spiritual leadership and guidance were required and were soon to be provided with the advent of Elijah, one of the most outstanding prophets of the Old Testament.

Elijah the Tishbite

In I Kings 17:1, we read that "Elijah the Tishbite, who was of the inhabitants of Gilead, said unto Ahab, As the Lord God of Israel liveth, before whom I stand, there shall not be dew nor rain these years, but according to my word."

Brief though this introduction is, it casts light upon the significance of this brave and rugged seer. The fact that he is called "the Tishbite" may suggest that he came from a town named Tishbe, although its position has not yet been positively identified. The reference to Gilead indicates that whether or not he was born to the east of Jordan, he had recently been living in that wild and picturesque area.

His opening announcement to Ahab, a king already notorious for his idolatrous practices (see I Kings 16:33), identifies Elijah as a true prophet who did not hesitate to challenge anyone who failed to obey the dictates of the Lord. Such a lengthy drought as he predicted had long been considered a sign of divine displeasure (see Deut. 11:16, 17). Elijah reminded Ahab of the inevitable effect of his conduct, adding that the prophet himself, as God's representative, could still remit or lessen the penalty if Ahab would but renounce his evil ways. Since the king remained obdurate, the devastating drought soon began to take effect.

Obeying the Lord's command, Elijah went to "the brook Cherith, that is before Jordan" (I Kings 17:3) — that is, in Gilead to the east of the river, an area already familiar to him. There he drank water from the brook, while according to the King James Version, he was fed by "ravens" (Hebrew, *oReBiM*) although the word could be read as *aRaBiM* (Arabs), since in early Hebrew writing only consonants appeared, the vowels being added by the reader or translator. Whether Elijah was fed by ravens or by friendly Arab tribesmen, his need was met.

Finally the brook dried up altogether, and the prophet was inspired to travel northwestward across Palestine to Zarephath — the Sarepta of the New Testament — near the Mediterranean port of Zidon (Sidon). Zarephath lay in a district governed by Ethbaal, father of Ahab's notorious wife, Jezebel; yet even there, in supposedly pagan territory, Elijah found not only food and water but also cooperation and receptivity conspicuously lacking among the Israelites.

On his arrival, Elijah encountered a widow, who, although she and her son appeared to be on the brink of starvation, lovingly shared what she had with the prophet. Her reward came promptly. She accepted Elijah's assurance that "the Lord God of Israel" (verse 14) would meet her need, and her apparently limited supply of meal and oil was quickly proved to be limitless. "And she, and he, and her house, did eat many days" (verse 15).

Before the prophet left the widow's home, her son fell dangerously ill and apparently expired. Faced by this new emergency, Elijah carried the boy to an upper room, where he himself lodged, and turned to God in prayer. The response to his petition was swift and effective, for we read that "the soul of the child came into him again, and he revived" (verse 22), and the prophet had the joy of returning him to his mother, alive and well. "Now by this I know," she cried, "that thou art a man of God, and that the word of the Lord in thy mouth is truth" (verse 24).

Elijah's Stand at Mount Carmel

Following his raising of the widow's son, Elijah remained at Zarephath until almost three years had passed since he had first warned King Ahab of the impending drought (see I Kings 17:1; 18:1). Meanwhile it had become increasingly severe, and Ahab's pagan wife, Jezebel, far from evidencing conversion or repentance, had slain many of the Israelite prophets (see I Kings 18:13); but the special object of her wrath was Elijah.

Yet when he was called by the Lord to "Go, shew thyself unto Ahab" (verse 1), neither fear nor danger deterred Elijah from obeying. Meeting a friend and supporter named Obadiah, the chief steward of Ahab's household, he insisted on having an audience with the king. Obadiah agreed, though he feared that dire results would surely follow (see I Kings 18:7–16). (This Obadiah should not be confused with the later "Writing Prophet" of that name.)

When the two men met, Ahab accused Elijah of being the one "that troubleth Israel"; but the prophet directly reversed the charge against him by affirming, "I have not troubled Israel; but thou, and thy father's house, in that ye have forsaken the commandments of the Lord, and thou hast followed Baalim" (verses 17, 18).

The efficacy of the prophet's divinely supported authority is proved by the fact that when he demanded that all the king's subjects appear on Mount Carmel, together with four hundred and fifty false prophets who upheld the pagan deity Baal, and some four hundred others supported and sponsored by Jezebel, Ahab immediately implemented his demand (see verse 20).

It was then that Elijah made his memorable plea for complete and wholehearted loyalty to the true God of Israel. According to the King James translation, he cried, "How long halt ye between two opinions?" Since in more modern English the Hebrew verb here means to "limp" or to "hobble," Elijah was surely warning the people against a wavering faith in God — an uncertain or partial allegiance to Him. A prompt and clear-cut decision was requisite: "If the Lord be God, follow him: but if Baal, then follow him" (verse 21).

In testing Elijah's challenge the prophets of Baal were to prepare a bullock for sacrifice, calling upon their alleged gods to burn it by providing fire from heaven. Hour after hour they prayed, but their prayers were completely unavailing: "there was neither voice, nor any to answer, nor any that regarded" (verse 29).

Thereupon Elijah rebuilt the altar of the Lord, which had fallen into disrepair, surrounding it with a deep trench and covering the wood used for fuel with pieces of another bullock, then drenching the whole area with no fewer than twelve barrels of the water so scarce in that time of drought (see verses 30–35).

In response to Elijah's fervent petition "the fire of the Lord fell, and consumed the burnt sacrifice, and the wood, and the stones, and the dust, and licked up the water that was in the trench" (verse 38); while the false prophets were quickly slain.

At last the people were convinced of the presence and power of Elijah's God, twice affirming that "The Lord, he is the God" (verse 39). Now that they were renouncing idolatry, the cause of the drought had been removed, and the rain soon fell in torrents (see verse 45).

Elijah at Mount Horeb

Valiant as had been Elijah's stand for unwavering loyalty to the true God on the slopes of Mount Carmel, and his equally forthright destruction of the leaders of paganism following that event, he was challenged by a further test. The anger of Jezebel became even more bitter against him, and he was forced to flee the country.

In his flight from Israel, Elijah traveled southward through Judah to Beersheba, its southern extremity, leaving his servant there and proceeding still farther into the wilderness for "a day's journey" (I Kings 19:4), a space of uncertain length, generally varying in accord with the capacity of the traveler. There he rested in the shadow of a "juniper tree," often understood as being an isolated bush of desert broom, where, in utter discouragement, he prayed for death to end his troubles.

But his great career was by no means over. On previous occasions (cf. 17:6, 10–15) food and drink had been provided from unexpected sources. Now Elijah was twice awakened by an angel who showed him bread and water prepared for him and encouraged him to follow in the footsteps of Moses — "unto Horeb the mount of God" (19:8; cf. Ex. 3:1).

Arriving at Horeb (also known as Sinai), the prophet lodged in a cave, there to await another experience of deep spiritual import. The reason for his coming was promptly demanded by God Himself. "Behold, the word of the Lord came to him, and he said unto him, What doest thou here, Elijah?" (I Kings 19:9.)

Elijah quickly reported his jealousy (or, more strictly, "zeal") on behalf of the Lord Himself, which had been countered by constant opposition from the children of Israel. He was, he contended, the only true Israelite prophet left in the land, and his own life was in imminent danger.

To this plea no direct response was forthcoming, although he was told to abandon his sheltering cave and to face the Lord Himself. "And, behold," the account continues, "the Lord passed by" (verse 11). The prophet experienced a terrible wind that shattered the mountains and rent the rocks before the Lord; but he found no trace of God in this phenomenon. It was followed by an earthquake and by a fire; but still Elijah waited for the Lord's response. At last he heard what the King James Version calls "a still small voice" (verse 12). The margin of the American Standard Version offers "a sound of gentle stillness."

The prophet then heard God's message coming to him first in the identical words that had introduced this experience, "What doest thou here, Elijah?" while he himself repeated almost word for word his former complaint (verses 13, 14).

Elijah was now called upon to continue his prophetic work even more actively than before. He was assured that, so far from being the only true prophet left in the land, he could count on some seven thousand loyal and active Israelites, who, while not necessarily prophets themselves, had not succumbed to the degrading influence of Baal or bowed down before him (see verse 18).

What must have encouraged Elijah still further was the promise that from now on he was to have aid in performing his arduous task. On leaving Horeb he was to anoint Elisha to be his assistant and his successor. Further aid in the banishment of idolatry would come through Hazael and Jehu, soon to become rulers of Syria and Israel respectively (see verses 15–17).

Elijah and His Successor

After his exalting converse with God on Mount Horeb, Elijah set out, encouraged by the assurance that he was not alone and would soon encounter Elisha, who would cooperate with and eventually succeed him.

Elisha and his parents lived at Abelmeholah in northern Israel, several miles west of the Jordan River. Since the Hebrew word *abel* means "meadow," it was probably an agricultural community. Indeed it is clear that Elisha was a successful young farmer when Elijah met him, for he was plowing a field large enough to justify the use of "twelve yoke of oxen" (I Kings 19:19), which he handled at one time.

Elijah was passing by en route from Mount Horeb to distant Damascus (see verse 15) when he met Elisha. Realizing intuitively that this must be the man whom God had ordained to succeed him, he "cast his mantle upon him" (verse 19). In Bible times, and especially in this context, a prophet's mantle was considered as symbolizing his mission or authority. Apparently no word was uttered on this momentous occasion; but Elisha instantly grasped and accepted the significance of the elder prophet's action. He ran after Elijah, who had already proceeded on his way, asking but one favor, namely, that he might bid farewell to his parents before following him.

The fact that Elisha promptly slew a pair of oxen and prepared a farewell feast for his friends, using as fuel "the instruments of the oxen" (verse 21) — presumably the yokes, the harness, the oxgoads, and so forth — suggests his readiness to renounce his former work and commence his prophetic mission.

While it is implied that the two men worked together during Elisha's period of training, the Bible record does not indicate directly how or where this was done; but when Elijah's earthly mission was drawing to a close, we find a vivid account of the understanding and cooperation between these outstanding seers. "It came to pass, when the Lord would take up Elijah into heaven by a whirlwind, that Elijah went with Elisha from Gilgal" (II Kings 2:1).

Repeatedly on this memorable journey Elijah tested the young man's loyalty and persistence. He suggested that he remain behind at Gilgal, at Bethel, or at Jericho; but on each occasion Elisha staunchly refused, crying, "As the Lord liveth, and as thy soul liveth, I will not leave thee" (verses 2, 4, and 6). Soon they came to the Jordan, where Elisha received a further justification of the stand he had taken. Elijah "took his mantle, and wrapped it together, and smote the waters" (verse 8), which parted before them, enabling them to cross dry-shod.

Apparently now fully convinced of Elisha's loyalty, Elijah offered his successor whatever parting gift he might suggest.

Elisha's request was a daring one — "a hard thing," as Elijah described it — for he asked for "a double portion" of the "spirit" shown by Elijah himself (verses 9, 10). Still

Elisha was assured that his plea would be answered if he saw Elijah when he was taken from him.

As the two friends conversed earnestly, the condition was fulfilled. "Behold, there appeared a chariot of fire, and horses of fire, and parted them both asunder; and Elijah went up by a whirlwind into heaven. And Elisha saw it, and he cried, My father, my father, the chariot of Israel, and the horsemen thereof" (II Kings 2:11, 12). Then he took up the mantle which had fallen from the shoulders of Elijah.

CHAPTER VIII ·

The Extension of Oral Prophecy

Elisha's Mission Takes Form

Following Elijah's translation, Elisha inherited his position and authority (see II Kings 2:15). While still in the vicinity of Jericho, he was called upon to deal with a problem that was troubling the people of that area. They reported that their city was indeed pleasant but claimed that "the water is naught, and the ground barren" (verse 19). Through the prophet's perception of the Lord's good will for the city, their need was swiftly and permanently met, an act that was to prove prophetic of many instances of aid, protection, and healing to be associated with the prophet's name.

Leaving Jericho, Elisha proceeded to Bethel. Here a strange incident occurred, which, as recorded in the King James Version, might appear to militate against the constructive kindliness of the prophet.

We read that, on his arrival, "little children . . . mocked him, and said unto him, Go up, thou bald head," whereupon the prophet "cursed them in the name of the Lord," and shortly they were destroyed by bears (verses 23, 24).

In the idiom of the Hebrew, the so-called "little children" might well be skeptical young men in their late teens. To call a man of that period "bald-headed" often implied either physical or moral leprosy. And the reference to Elisha going "up" was doubtless a sneering allusion to Elijah's departure, recently witnessed by Elisha (see verses 11, 12). Bethel itself, where the present incident occurred, had become a center of pagan worship (see I Kings 12:32).

The ensuing punishment may appear unduly severe, but the young men involved were surely old enough to know better than to scorn the inspired activities of both Elijah and Elisha. Elisha may well have been present when Elijah sternly denounced Ahab and Jezebel for conniving at the murder of Naboth (see I Kings 21:17–19, 23) or when he assured Ahaziah that the king's accident would prove fatal because he sought for aid, not from the true God of Israel but from Baal-zebub, the pagan god of Ekron (see II Kings 1:2–4). It is understandable that he should act in conformity with the attitude of his great predecessor.

As Elisha's career continued, he was honored as a counselor of kings. When the rulers of Israel, Judah, and Edom were planning a campaign against the king of Moab, there was a severe drought (see II Kings 3:5–10). Bearing in mind the power shown by Elijah in his day, the Israelite king now turned to Elisha for help, assured that he also was guided by "the word of the Lord" (verses 11, 12). At his suggestion trenches were dug in the valleys and overnight were found to be overflowing with water. Thus the drought was broken.

Elisha was also noted for meeting the needs of sincere and

deserving individuals. On one such occasion he was approached by a bereaved widow, who assured him of the piety of her family. Now that her husband was no longer with her, she explained, a creditor was insisting that unless a debt was settled promptly, her two sons would be taken as slaves (see II Kings 4:1).

In response to the prophet's query (verse 2), "What hast thou in the house?" she reported that her limited assets were a single pot of oil. But when obediently and expectantly she borrowed empty vessels from all her neighbors, every pot was filled to overflowing from her own apparently tiny store. Obeying Elisha's advice, she sold the oil, paid her debt, and had enough left to feed herself and her family.

Elisha and the Shunammite

Elisha's healing work was an outstanding mark of his career, and much can be gained from considering his association with the brave Shunammite who is described as "a great woman" (II Kings 4:8). She recognized him as "an holy man of God" (verse 9), welcomed him as her guest on repeated occasions, and, with her husband, provided a special room for the prophet's use.

Grateful for her generosity, and learning that she was childless, he assured her that within a year she would bear a son, despite the fact that her husband, a prosperous farmer, was well on in years. Elisha's promise was at first more than she was prepared to accept, but in due course it was fulfilled.

One morning, several years later, the boy, who had joined his father in the harvest field, was suddenly stricken by severe pains in his head. Although promptly returned to his mother's care, about noon he passed away on her knee.

Placing the child on Elisha's bed, the Shunammite resolutely closed the door and set out to procure the prophet's aid. It is indicative of her firm faith and eager expectancy that she did not even share with her husband the nature of this emergency.

When he questioned her reason for an unexpected visit to their friend the prophet — since no special occasion seemed to warrant such a move — she reassured him by using that vivid and comforting Hebrew word *Shalom* — rendered "well" in verse 23 and again in verse 26 — although its literal meaning is "peace." Few words in the Hebrew language include such depth of meaning, implying as it does, not merely peace but also assurance, welfare, harmony, and even prosperity.

Hurrying westward across the fertile plain of Esdraelon, the woman approached Mount Carmel and was recognized in the distance by Elisha, who dispatched his servant to inquire about her welfare.

Her only reply came in the form of that great word *Shalom!* Peace! — the assurance that all was well. But when she reached Elisha, she fell at his feet in obvious distress.

Alert to her need, Elisha sent Gehazi to minister to the lad without delay, carrying the symbol of prophetic authority, the prophet's staff. On his arrival at the home Gehazi could find no response on the child's part. The servant reported, "The child is not awaked" (II Kings 4:31).

On the prophet's arrival at Shunem, "behold, the child was dead, and laid upon his bed" (verse 32). Here, indeed, was need for urgent and effective prayer. The prophet closed the door, remaining alone with the boy, and turned to God for aid. Within a short time his prayers were answered, and he had the joy of returning the lad to his mother, alive and well.

The sequel to this remarkable healing appears in a later chapter (II Kings 8), indicating Elisha's continued care for the Shunammite and her son. Convinced that a severe famine was imminent, he warned the family to leave the area. Obediently they did so, only to discover, on their return from Philistia seven years later, that their house and land had been forfeited.

To correct this injustice the Shunammite turned for aid to the king, who, in examining the case, learned from Gehazi that this was the woman whose son Elisha had raised from the dead, and both mother and son were on hand to confirm it. The Shunammite received complete restoration of her property by royal decree, while the prophet's fame continued to spread.

The Widening Scope of Elisha's Activities

The prophet Elisha seems to have brought aid and support to many people of Israel who came to him in trouble, but he did not limit his kindly ministrations to those of his own nation, as evidenced by his dealings with Naaman, a noted general in the army of the king of Syria.

In spite of his valor and his influence at court, Naaman was afflicted with the dread disease of leprosy. Knowing of her master's trouble, a young Israelite girl who had been taken captive by the Syrians and was now serving as a maid to Naaman's wife reported to her mistress what she had heard of Elisha's healing activities. In due course her kindly suggestion reached the ears both of the Syrian king and of his general.

Traveling in state and with the king's blessing, Naaman made the long journey from Damascus to Elisha's home in

Israel, obviously anticipating a royal reception and a swift healing administered by the prophet in person. But to Naaman's indignation Elisha did not even appear. He simply sent a message, promising Naaman that he would be healed on condition that he wash in the nearby River Jordan.

At first Naaman's national and personal pride resisted the application of this apparently simple remedy. To him, "Abana and Pharpar," the famous rivers that assured the fertility of the area surrounding Damascus, seemed far more important than any Israelite stream, "so he turned and went away in a rage" (II Kings 5:12). But before long he was prepared to comply with the sound advice of his servants that he should gratefully accept the prophet's offer. Receptivity replaced opposition and anger; pride gave way before humility. When at last he was ready to follow Elisha's explicit instructions, he washed seven times in the Jordan, "and his flesh came again like unto the flesh of a little child, and he was clean" (verse 14).

It is memorable that when Jesus asserted that "no prophet is accepted in his own country" (Luke 4:24), he supported his point by noting that while "many lepers were in Israel in the time of Eliseus" — an alternative spelling of "Elisha" — the only leper healed was Naaman the Syrian (verse 27).

Elisha seems to have been specially interested in training young men who were eager to share in the work of prophecy. Often called "sons of the prophets" (II Kings 4:38; 6:1, etc.), they were apparently not "sons" of the famed Old Testament seers in any literal sense but simply youths inspired by their example.

On one occasion, in the vicinity of Gilgal, Elisha met with a sizable group of these young men, who were "sitting before him," doubtless listening intently to his instruction (II Kings 4:38). Famine was at that time ravaging the area, and the prophet, generous as always, invited them all to dine with him, only to discover that someone had added to their fare a quantity of shredded gourds, evidently considered highly poisonous. The prophet simply added to it a little meal (see verse 41). The fears of his guests were swiftly quieted; and when they all ate together, no ill effects ensued.

Thus Elisha proved in advance the practicality of Christ Jesus' assurance in Mark's Gospel (16:18), "If they drink any deadly thing, it shall not hurt them."

Concluding Events in Elisha's Career

Elisha's strong interest in the work of "the sons of the prophets," and their loyalty to him, are indicated in a brief passage in II Kings 6:1–7. Noting that the area which they shared with Elisha was becoming too crowded, these eager young students proposed that their joint headquarters be moved closer to the Jordan River, assuring him that each of their members would cooperate in the work of construction. The prophet agreed. As one was felling timber for this purpose, the axhead fell into the stream, to his dismay, "for it was borrowed," but with Elisha's aid, he quickly retrieved it. "The iron did swim" (verses 5, 6).

Later, Elisha showed his alertness and prophetic insight in warning the king of Israel of the precise position which the Syrian king had chosen for his own camp in a projected attack on the Israelites. Thanks to the prophet's warning, the Israelite ruler was repeatedly enabled to defend himself and his nation successfully, while the Syrians made every effort to find and to destroy Elisha, learning that it was he who had discovered and divulged their supposedly secret plans (see verses 8–14).

Informed by his spies that the prophet was at Dothan, the Syrian ruler sent an army to surround the city by night; and when Elisha's servant awoke in the early morning, he was startled to discover that "an host compassed the city both with horses and chariots" (verse 15). His fears were silenced by his master's assurance that "they that be with us are more than they that be with them" (verse 16). Moreover, in response to Elisha's prayer, his servant no longer saw horses and chariots as symbols of danger or attack but rather as symbols of protection — "horses and chariots of fire round about Elisha" (verse 17).

The Syrians were turned from their purpose by temporary blindness; and when their sight returned, they found they had been led into Samaria by Elisha himself, who saw to it that they were amply fed and sent back to Syria unmolested — a generous act eventuating in the desired result that "the bands of Syria came no more into the land of Israel" (verse 23).

In a further scene, Elisha plays a leading part (see II Kings 13:14–19). By now he had been serving his country and its people for almost half a century; and his great career appeared to be approaching its end. As he lay in bed, he was visited by Joash, the young king of Israel, who wept at the possibility of Elisha's demise and said, "O my father, my father, the chariot of Israel, and the horsemen thereof" (verse 14), echoing the words Elisha himself had used when Elijah was translated (see 2:12).

On the present occasion, Elisha had Joash select a bow and arrows. One arrow was to be shot eastward through the open window, while the prophet placed his hands on those of the young king; and as the arrow sped on its way, Elisha explained its import — that the Syrian forces would be speedily defeated. Then Joash was to strike the ground with the remaining arrows. He did so three times, only to learn that had he continued to five or six times, the downfall of Syria would have been complete.

So with his country's interests foremost in his thought, Elisha passed away. While he is rarely mentioned directly in the New Testament, his wide concept of abundance, shown in II Kings 4:42–44, where he fed "an hundred men" from a very small supply of food, prepared in some respects for John 6:8–13 and other Gospel passages.

CHAPTER IX ·

The Dawning Influence of Prophecy on the Law

"J": A Primitive Source of the Pentateuch

The outstanding work of the prophets Elijah and Elisha in the ninth century B.C. provided a vital development in the progress of the Hebrew people. With Amos and Hosea, Isaiah of Jerusalem, and Micah in the eighth century, *written* prophecy began, continuing in almost unbroken succession for some six centuries.

Before we approach this further unfoldment, let us consider a parallel contribution already under way when the ninth century prophets were performing their own important task.

The first five books of the Bible, the Pentateuch (literally, "the five-fold volume"), were long credited exclusively to Moses, their central figure. During the past hundred years or more, however, an increasing number of Biblical scholars noted discrepancies between the two accounts of creation.

Others observed variations between the two accounts of the Flood (e.g. Gen. 6:19 and 7:2), conflicting accounts of the acts and attitudes of the patriarchs, and so forth. Such views uphold the now generally accepted hypothesis that the Pentateuch is not the work of one individual but contains several different sources.

The earliest significant source to be found in the Pentateuch, and even beyond it, is generally described as the Jehovistic, or Judean, source. It uses Jehovah — variously spelled as Yahweh or Yahwah and termed "Lord" in the English Bible — as its distinctive name for Deity; and because of its many references to Judean place names, was evidently written in Judah, the southern part of Palestine. Bible students use J as a symbol of this source.

After the children of Israel had escaped from their bondage in Egypt, eventually to reach the Promised Land of Canaan, it was still many years before they became firmly settled there. The Philistines made war upon them, and even Saul, their first king, met with a series of reverses. But with David's accession to the throne and the growing power and influence of his son and successor, Solomon, there developed in them a national consciousness, a desire to record the history of their people. David prepared the way for this by appointing a "recorder" and a "scribe" (II Sam. 20:24, 25).

Sometime in the ninth century B.C., in the days of Elijah and Elisha, the Jehovistic Biblical source known as J seems to have been prepared. The historical period that it covered cannot be precisely defined, but it started with an allegorical account of creation as material, the story of Adam and Eve. Commencing with Genesis 2:4, the J source contributes to much of that book and appears at intervals down to the reign of David.

While one may readily question the anthropomorphisms and limitations of J's account of the "Lord God" and His reputed formation of man from "the dust of the ground" (Gen. 2:7), the vividness of the writer's style remains one of his most distinctive characteristics. His religious and moral ideas may appear limited, but for his day he was an advanced thinker, presenting an early philosophy of history. His character studies of Adam and Eve, Cain and Abel, Jacob and Rachel, and many others, are unforgettable.

The work of another writer or writers who used the Hebrew name *Elohim* (God) in the first chapter of Genesis and elsewhere provided a higher concept of Deity and of creation.

"E": An Elohistic Source of the Pentateuch

In a previous passage, mention was made of the primitive source often called "J," written in Judah and stressing the term Jehovah, one of the spellings used for Yahweh or Yahwah, often translated Lord. This is the name for Deity so characteristic of the account of creation that begins in the second chapter of Genesis, from verse 4 onward. Its use continues in Chapter 3 and in later passages.

The source now under consideration is generally referred to as "E." This source is thought to have been written in the northern kingdom of Ephraim, or Israel. It chose to lay special emphasis on the deeply significant Hebrew word *Elohim,* repeatedly translated "God."

Elohim is the term for "God" used in the familiar and deeply loved first chapter of Genesis, so justly considered as presenting the spiritual record of creation — the God who "created man in his own image, in the image of God created he him" (verse 27). It is generally held, however, that the first chapter of Genesis belongs to still another body of material, often designated "P," and that a writer or writers of a priestly background prepared its memorable and beautiful phrases at a later date, perhaps soon after the Exile in Babylon.

It seems likely that the Elohistic writer, who was probably an Ephraimite, was strongly influenced by the thought of the prophets, and especially perhaps by Elisha, who was himself a resident of the northern kingdom and must have worked with many young prophets living in that area, whether at Bethel (see II Kings 2:3) or at Gilgal (see 4:38). This need not, of course, imply that Elisha himself wrote this source, but it may well have been prepared or sponsored by one of his disciples. The writer or compiler of this E source has no hesitation in implying that both Abraham and Moses were prophets (see Gen. 20:2, 7; Num. 11:29).

The results of this strong prophetic influence are readily noticeable. In the earlier Jehovistic source, known as J, "the Lord" is conceived of as walking and even as fighting with men (see Gen. 3:8; Ex. 4:24); but in the present Elohistic account, *Elohim* (God) is viewed as communing with men, not personally or directly, but through angels, visions, or dreams (see Gen. 28:12).

In the Jehovistic source, which often appears more primitive, Abram is shown as readily permitting his wife to drive Hagar out into the wilderness, in spite of the impending birth of Ishmael (see Gen. 16:6). But in the more kindly E source, the patriarch is represented as being grieved at Sarah's anger; Hagar is not dismissed until the baby is weaned; and she and her child receive water and provisions for their journey (see Gen. 21:8–14).

Another important point with regard to this early Elohistic source, E, is that it is considered to include the Decalogue, or Ten Commandments, as found in Exodus 20. It is clear that these early prophetic historians showed a definite interest in law as it was accepted and practiced.

The Old Testament World

HITTITE EMPIRE
TAURUS MTS.
Carchemish
Hara
PADAN-ARAM
CYPRUS
Ugarit
SYRIA
Hamath
Arvad
Tadm
Palmy
Byblos
Sidon
Mediterranean Sea
Damascus
Tyre
Hazor
ISRAEL
Shechem
Bethel
AMMON
Jericho
Jerusalem
Ashkelon
JUDAH
Dead (salt) Sea
MOAB
Mendes
Tanis
GOSHEN
Beersheba
EDOM
Kadesh-barnea
EGYPT
Pyramids
Memphis
Lisht
Nile R.
SINAI PENINSULA
Gulf of Aqaba
Mt. Sinai
Red Sea